CW01510134

TOTAL
INNOVATION

TOTAL INNOVATION

How to Develop the Products that your Customers want

Stewart Bray

FT
PITMAN
PUBLISHING

PITMAN PUBLISHING
128 Long Acre, London WC2E 9AN

A Division of Pearson Professional Limited

First published in Great Britain 1995

British Library Cataloguing in Publication Data
A CIP catalogue record for this book can be obtained
from the British Library.

ISBN 0273 61261 1

1 3 5 7 9 10 8 6 4 2

Typeset by Northern Phototypesetting Co. Ltd, Bolton
Printed and bound in Great Britain by
Biddles Ltd, Guildford and King's Lynn

*The Publishers' policy is to use paper manufactured
from sustainable forests.*

CONTENTS

1

INTRODUCTION

'Europe's lack of competitiveness is not simply the result of high labour costs'

EC Industry commissioner

'A lack of innovation, up-to-date infrastructure, and efficient decision making were as important in determining competitiveness'

Mr Martin Banglemann *(The Daily Telegraph* 15/9/1994)

The object of this book is to encourage companies to create a climate which rewards innovation, and to establish a framework for the development and innovation of new products and services and to institute a New Products Scheme which sets out the needed infrastructure and ensures rapid and effective decision taking, increasing the companies' competitive edge.

THE CONCEPT OF INNOVATION

The British are, by nature, innovative. Some of the most important inventions in terms of advances in the human condition have been produced by individuals and companies on these shores. Innovation is not only about invention; it is about the commercial application of knowledge or techniques in new ways or for new purposes. It is important in every business, small, medium and large. It is not necessarily about thinking up new things in the first place, but about exploiting opportunities profitably, and ahead of rivals.

The concept of innovation means some basic rethinking of a company's activities:

- Managing change to allow new ideas, new technologies, new techniques or even opportunities to flourish
- Improving the applications of emerging technologies, new skills, processes and services to provide competitive advantage and thus to increase profits
- Improving aspects of research, development, design, market research, customer interaction, customer care, marketing and quality control
- Encouraging new ideas, adopting and adapting them to improve the company's competitive position
- Accepting that regardless of size, or type of business, any business can innovate and increase its profits, customer base and competitive position
- Altering the company mentality to become more receptive to new ideas, and build on ideas and experience to the common good. To qualify such ideas to ensure that they are sound and will increase the business opportunity.

However, it is almost impossible to make someone innovate at the drop of a hat. It is widely assumed that the research and development department is responsible for new products and innovation and that one of the measures of innovation within companies is the amount of money that it spent on R&D. However this is a widely misleading concept.

The reason is that innovation is not invention. Innovation is the process that takes an idea, and successfully markets it to such an extent that its concept becomes an accepted player in the marketplace. Innovation is a companywide process that involves all disciplines and facets within a company and is not exclusive to the R&D department. Many successful innovations are conceived by individuals who remain frustrated by a particular product or service, and so seek to improve it. In doing so, they launch a process whereby commercial advantage takes place and the product becomes a significant generator of revenue. Innovation can be evolutionary, or revolutionary. For example, the motor car has slowly improved over the last 50 years with a host of features such as safety, reliability, cost, comfort and fuel efficiency. The establishment of cellular telephone systems has revolutionised the telecommunications business to such an extent that some developing countries, have relied on this innovation and have largely ignored the older 'copper wire' type of telephone system. Thailand has, for example ten times as many cellular telephones as traditional ones.

Some companies are very good at innovation. Hewlett-Packard, the computer company, has moved relentlessly on having out-performed all its rivals by producing a constant stream of world-beating new products. This has not occurred by chance; it has happened because the management of Hewlett-Packard actively encourages the innovation process and is intimately involved in the process. Many major companies such as Hewlett-Packard and ICI use a 'New Products Scheme', which greatly aids the innovation process and accelerates product development. Many other companies use some form of product evaluation.

If a company wants to be innovative, it has to provide a forum for its staff to provide new ideas, and for those ideas to be nurtured, sorted, encouraged, discarded, tested, and commercialised. This starts with the chairman, and finishes with the newest employee. The object of this book is to show you how to develop a framework as a New Product Scheme, that is applicable to any size of company. It is designed to provide accelerated development of new ideas, and to sort out the runners from the non-runners, so that the company can devote its resources to those new products which can succeed. The New Products Scheme also helps with decision taking; if the right information is provided to assist the decision, then the quicker the process.

MANAGING CHANGE

Inevitably, there is a 'Luddite' element in any company which will resist the idea that innovation can be a companywide concept. When they trained 30 years ago it was up to the 'R&D boys and the lads from the drawing office'. That may be so, but times, competition and necessity have moved on. Successful and innovative companies have an enthusiastic approach to new ideas, and tend to be supportive of new concepts however 'off the wall'. It is apparent that such companies enjoy a management which succours and encourages such ideas. Managers encourage and support juniors in their departments, as mentors, and do not try to hog the limelight, or claim the idea as being their own. If a New Product Scheme is being introduced it must be implemented from the top. It must be sold to the workforce in the same way as quality or safety is, and it must become a way of business life.

MARKETING – A TOOL FOR ALL COMPANIES

One of the most frequent observations is that Britain has a record second to none for its invention, new ideas, patents and designs, and yet fails to make a commercial success of such ideas. Items such as the swing wing, television, the transistor, penicillin, etc., are often quoted as British ideas whose major success has been overseas. One of the fundamental problems seems to be the compartmentalisation of departments within companies, and the lack of enthusiasm to cross-fertilise ideas between departments. Any inventor has to be able to conceptualise his idea and then sell it to third parties. In doing so he is unwittingly acting as a salesperson, and many inventors would feel insulted if they were equated with salespeople. However, this is exactly what is necessary and, to put it bluntly, if a company does not sell its wares, then it does not exist. The wise practitioner, knowing that his strengths are as a designer, will allow another to evangelise his idea, knowing that his own selling skills are limited. It is much better to get an advocate for the product, whose skills are to sell the idea of the product. If a product is a commercial success when sold overseas by a third party, but not when controlled by the designer's company there is probably one major skill lacking. That skill is a lack of vision.

All new products need to be associated with a vision element, and need to be sold as enthusiastically to company members as to customers. If you were approached by a colleague and invited to see a demonstration of what 'could be the next major product in the company', you are hardly likely to refuse. You may hate the sight of your colleague, but you cannot deny that you are intrigued and it is this intrigue which will have drawn you to see the product. Your personal feelings will not cloud your reception of the idea. Comments like 'this product will double the company's turnover' have a conversation-stopping element, and they certainly attract attention.

It seems, therefore, that the development of new products needs a combination of experience, radicality, missionary zeal and a very thick skin. It is one of the most important elements of a company's activities. It needs to be encouraged and nurtured, and above all it needs to be done properly. Every employee should be encouraged to think up new ideas and new ideas should not be regarded as the exclusive right of the R&D department.

The author attended a meeting about a completely new vehicle immobiliser system with a third-party supplier. The inventor explained his idea to the supplier and showed his prototype, whereupon the supplier's engineering director launched a serious attack on the idea and produced a whole series of supposed weaknesses. The inventor stood his ground and slowly and patiently explained how he had already designed his system to overcome the alleged weaknesses. As the invention involved cars, and a majority of the population drive a car, anyone who drives a car becomes an expert and thus will comment. Why a supplier, who has only met the inventor for a period of minutes should launch into such an attack, without really understanding the product or its features, and should feel that he has any right to make comments at that stage, is a mystery. However, it is a common fact that many people will oppose a new idea, probably because it is new and has an element of the unknown.

In another company, a proposer, having had a rough time within his own company, turned up in steel helmet and flak jacket! He got his message across. If people are prepared to put time and effort into thinking out new ideas, at least we should have the manners and good sense to hear them out. The most common comment that innovators hear about products which are designed for new markets is that there is 'no demand'. Akio Morita, the Chairman of Sony, heard this from his own marketing department, when considering the design of the Walkman. He wisely ignored the comment.

In 1989, I was returning from Comdex in Las Vegas, where ICI were exhibiting an innovation in the colour printing world of computers, when I met an engineering professor at Caltech. While discussing the ICI project he asked why it was that Britain was one of the most innovative nations on the planet and yet their inventions were largely commercialised by other countries. In all honesty I said I had no idea, and today I still do not! However, I do believe that vision is an important element, which allows individuals and groups of innovators to look to the future. To that end it is the marketing department which should be looking for new products or services, in order to expand the company's long-term product portfolio and hence its business base.

Ask yourself a simple question. 'What will I be doing in the company in five years' time, and what products will the company be selling?' If your vision of your company looks a bit bleak, if there is a distinct lack of new products being developed, is it not time you did something about it?

All companies have a marketing department, and each company has ideas as to what it thinks marketing should be. Few Western companies have 'new products' departments, or even a 'director of new products'. They tend to have compartmentalised departments which interact, and some better than others. The Japanese have new product departments, and often have departments called 'Second Marketing Section' which, having been literally translated from the Japanese, often indicate that the department is involved in new products.

In the United States, a recent survey sent to a random selection of chief executives from small, medium and large companies, shows that very little effort is made formally to develop new products. Of the 10 most important activities listed by the CEOs only 7 per cent listed developing new products, while 81 per cent listed sexual equality in the workplace. Most made passing reference to research, but research as such does not produce new products, it merely acts as a catalyst to the rest of the company.

This is a staggering survey, and while it does not speak for any particular industry or company, it poses the question as to how the CEOs in the 93 per cent of companies who did not regard developing new products as being particularly important, expect their companies to survive in the long term.

The Harvard Business School reports that its graduates regard the production of new products as being the essential driver to a successful business. It is therefore difficult to understand why the captains of industry do not give more emphasis to product development, as this is surely one of the single most important activities that a company can do to survive and thrive. It is interesting to look at new entrants to the US or UK stock markets. They tend to be young, innovative companies, usually with a limited product range. Their ability to grow and flourish depends on their growth of new products, and broadening of their product range.

In Britain, a great deal of time is spent on training with regard to 'quality'. There is no doubt that this is a very important issue and that bad quality can cause companies to lose customers. However, it is rare that bad quality means make or break for a company's survival. If a company produces a series of failed new products, then it is not likely to survive. If a company fails to produce new products, and 'cash cows' existing products, it will eventually wither and die. It is believed that a new products philosophy should be as ingrained into the working practices of the company, in the same way that quality is. As much time should be devoted to training on new products development as quality training. Innovation depends on a number of basic building blocks. These can be defined as the fertile ground in which to nurture new ideas, and the ability of all managers to help and advise innovators to advance their ideas is something which could advance the future of the company.

Unfortunately you cannot go to a group of employees and say 'design a new product by this time next week' any more than you can expect a painter to produce a masterpiece on demand. Many new products result from a series of chance conversations between individuals, some of whom would not normally be associated with new products (i.e. they are not in the R&D department). What is necessary is a companywide platform for new ideas to be sympathetically received and compared on a like-for-like basis. Any employee should be entitled to contribute regardless of job title or department.

Generally, a small initial team, which develops the new idea, will be more likely to lead the product to a stage where it succeeds. This is because the thought processes are tightly focused, common views abound within the team, and the team is able to work fast to advance the idea or project. Some larger companies allow their employees to spend up to 10 per cent of their time on researching new ideas, or innovations, and actively encourage it. Results suggest that this time is not abused.

I am often asked what would happen if there was no marketing in Western society. My answer is simple – Russia. Any visitor to Russia will depart with the lasting impression of long queues, no consumer products, no choice, and often nothing at all, because no demand has been forecast and so nothing has been made!

Marketing is seen as a 'black art' and marketeers are blamed for any consumer phenomenon from cellular telephones, video games, and the rise and fall of the skateboard. Many newspapers use the word to indicate the selling process, with phrases such as the 'marketing of gas'. This actually means the selling of gas to a captive market with no direct competition from other gas suppliers.

Most people are very unclear as to what they mean (or think they mean) when they use the word 'marketing'. I have heard many definitions of marketing and like none of them. I believe that a marketing operation produces:

1 The *Right* Product
2 At the *Right* Price
3 At the *Right* Time
4 With the *Right* Production
5 With the *Right* Positioning.

Most good marketing operations are producing many products all meeting the above criteria. Many small companies produce outstanding products and there is evidence that a small tight-knit group often produces better, more clearly perceived products than their larger rivals. Smaller groups react faster, and do not have to negotiate their individual time allocations as do larger groups. Smaller groups also work harder and devote longer hours to their 'baby'.

LOOKING FROM ANOTHER VIEW

If the implications of the above statements are considered, the marketing department must be capable of market research, have an in-depth technical knowledge of its product range, and that of its competitors, must be capable of R&D, productionisation, production, finance and packaging ... and that is before anything is actually made! In a lot of companies the marketing department is one person!

The marketing department, to a certain extent must be likened to the conductor of the orchestra. Like a conductor, it must understand the business, and be capable of understanding most of the operations which make the business work. It must act as the co-ordinator of a whole range of business activities, so that the product arrives to meet the '5 R' criteria mentioned above. If a conductor calls for the strings to start a phrase before the wind section has finished its section, the result sounds a mess, and the audience quite rightly votes with its feet. The same applies with companies, except that the stakes are 10,000 times higher. Success or failure can often depend on one key decision which can be pivotal to the company's future. For example, Rolls-Royce in the 1970s was brought down by the decision to develop the RB211 jet engine. The decision to proceed was undoubtedly correct. *What was not understood was the financial demands that the development had on the cash flow of the company.*

Many companies produce new products which have come from R&D or from engineering and if this method is successful, then there is no reason to change the core teams. If the products are less than successful, or need to be modified in order to become successful, then thought must be given to the customer element. This should be via the marketing department.

Most companies do regular marketing, but many do not call it that! Smaller companies develop new products, and most do mailshots, exhibitions and attend seminars. They discuss new concepts with customers, look at what their competitors are doing and test their products in the marketplace. This book is just as much for them as for the bigger companies who have marketing departments and budgets to match.

What is very plain is that almost all companies could do better. Those that do well, producing a constant stream of new products, tend to perform well in the long term. With the current recession it is interesting to look at Stock Exchange results for the players in a given field. If the general trend is for lower profits, or even losses, the exception to the rule pops up, and invariably has weathered the storms by producing new products, even in a recession-hit market. Many companies produce outstanding new products when young and then fail to produce products to replace them, so that they wither and fade.

THE MICROCOMPUTER STORY

The development of the microcomputer is a classic example of how new products transform companies in a few years, often for them to fade quite quickly. Commodore, for example, once had the European microcomputer market almost sewn up with the Pet. They failed to follow on and allowed other companies to produce rival products, ultimately resulting in IBM joining the fray. Even IBM could not stay the pace, and having enjoyed 30 per cent market share at one time, their global market share is now about 11 per cent. The study of the microcomputer market should be required by all marketing personnel, simply because there are so many lessons to be learned. Product development and how a product can change the marketplace are important lessons to be learned. This, in turn, ultimately changes the way the market does business. In ten years the microcomputer has gone from a hi-tech piece of computer wizardry to a commodity that is sold like a radio or washing machine. Only companies that can manage the dynamic change can survive. Most computer companies these days expect their product life cycle to be as short as six months. Their new products departments are producing the next product, then the one after that, and starting the R&D for the next follow-on product. I regard the microcomputer marketplace as being one of the most challenging that has ever existed. There is a relentless drive for newer electronics, resulting in faster and cheaper products. If you suggested to the Production Director of Ford UK, that his next Ford Escort would have to be twice as powerful, at half the price, he would invite you to leave the room. In the microcomputer market this is exactly what happens. In the early days, companies had to be backed up with strong sales support, and strong service support, resulting in high personnel budgets. Now, the microcomputer is sold as a consumer product in the same way as a microwave or television set. Company structures are totally different, and so are the marketplaces and distribution systems that serve them. Only the strong and the flexible survive, and most are high-volume-low-cost operations.

OBJECTIVES OF THE BOOK

The objectives of this book are to inspire a different way of developing new products, to formalise an informal way for personnel to nurture their pet ideas and to ensure that they get a sympathetic hearing. To establish a level playing field for new ideas to be compared, evaluated and tested; to establish a means whereby a company, be it small or large, gets new ideas qualified. In return, it allows its staff, from the Managing Director to the office boy, the time and resources to expand the idea into a product, to the mutual advantage of all. If a new product is to develop, almost all the departments of a company will be involved. Their collective input will enhance and change the original idea, but the result will be workable and saleable.

It is suggested that if a New Product Scheme is set up, and adopted, there is a set of basic ground rules which everyone in the company can understand. Perhaps it may be worth thinking about setting up a 'New Products Department', if the company is large enough. Smaller companies may like to reflect on the ideas of 'New Products Groups' that can be anything from a few interested parties 'shooting the breeze' to full-blown committees producing new ideas. Very small companies will not need such formality. What they need is a checklist of actions in order to ensure that nothing is forgotten, and that the limited money and time is best allocated to ensure success.

What is vital is that senior management understands that the company will not compete in its marketplace unless it produces new products. For example, the advertising industry tends to be constantly changing its companies and partnerships. The reason for this is the constant change within the industry itself, resulting in disaffected managers establishing their own businesses. If the disaffection had been removed, the manager would have been an asset to his old employer – now he is a threat and a competitor. What is equally as important is the understanding that the majority of new products will ultimately fail for one reason or another. The key to the success of developing a new product is to get it right, and the whole objective of a New Product Scheme is to help in doing exactly that.

CAUTIONARY TALE

A well-known Japanese company with a long-term reputation in the market launched a 'cold fusion laser printer'. The key feature was to allow printing from computers without heat and thus not producing harmful ozone (a by-product of xerography and laser printers). The product failed, because the print fell off the page if the paper was handled, folded or dropped. The manufacturer withdrew the product, and ten years later still has very limited credibility in that sector of the market.

COMMENT

*The product failed the **Right Product** test. It was never a product because it could not compete with xerography. If properly field tested, it would never had been allowed out of the R&D department as it did not meet normal customer expectations and would not compete with rivals.*

LESSONS TO BE LEARNED

During the course of the book, we shall be looking at a number of cautionary tales which represent billions of pounds of investment, research, lost sales and promotion of new products to the betterment of the rivals, or loss of the taxpayers' money. They also represent lost opportunities to develop other products which may well have succeeded where these have failed.

The message must be clear. A simple New Product Scheme would have applied corrective action to each case and would have either killed off the project at an early stage, modified it in light of customer comment, or user experience, or ensured that the product was at the right place at the right time, with the right volumes. Many companies still insist on 'research-led' products, and these products often fail because of a perception failure in the design of the product. Market-led products are much less likely to fail, because customer interaction will have weeded out wrong designs and bad development before costs become expensive.

THE ALTERNATIVES

Any company, small, medium or large, must innovate and in doing so must produce new products thereby investing in money, resources and time. Few companies can back every potential new product and therefore must undergo a selection procedure. If they choose wrongly, then they have wasted vital time, money and resources which could have been put into a successful alternative product and they have also, unwittingly, given much help to their competitors because their activity in the market-place has raised the expectations of the customer base. The message is simple – you must get it right first time!

WEEDING OUT

One of the key skills of successful innovation is the ability to weed out the non-runners, the non-starters, and the also-rans, from the real winners, so that the company's money, time and resources are concentrated onto products which will become part of the company's future and which will contribute to the company's ongoing overheads and provide long-term profits. There are skills which can be learned, and which can help senior managers to weed out the possible from the probable.

THE HUMAN ELEMENT

In addition, from a human perspective, it is very important to encourage innovative thinking and to ensure that ideas from innovators are not dismissed out of hand. A structured New Product Scheme gives a common framework for innovation and encourages new ideas, but allows the wheat and chaff to be separated without offence. The New Products Scheme also produces a stream of innovative ideas to be discussed and disseminated throughout the company, increasing the teamwork approach to the company's future prospects. The New Products Scheme needs to be understood from top to bottom of the company and will provide a clear avenue for ideas. Some may never become new products, but may alter the shape of existing working practices or existing products, simply because there is a route which understands and recognises an idea that will improve an existing condition and in so doing increases the competitive edge.

David Allen, in his book *Developing Successful New Products* (Pitman Publishing, 1994), indicates from his experience in the car industry, that interdepartmental rivalry can kill off a product or project. This is clearly unacceptable, as each idea must be given the same impartial hearing, as this is in the company's interest. All senior staff must be able to mould and shape ideas which involve their departments, even if the idea has originated elsewhere. In traditionally structured companies, each department has line responsibility and ideas which come from other departments are viewed with considerable scepticism. The NIH philosophy prevails – Not

Invented Here. The New Products Scheme is designed to encourage cross-departmental teams, and for them to succeed it is important that support comes from each department, and that progress is regularly reported to all the departments. Department heads are much more likely to view a product favourably, and become supporters of it if one of their members, for whom they have budget responsibility, is able to demonstrate that the product is progressing. Once a new product scheme is implemented, the successful launch of the first new product results in the second product development running much more smoothly. It proves that accountants, engineers, production people and even salespeople can work as a team.

2

FROM IDEA TO PRODUCT

THE HORROR STORIES

Literally thousands of new products are launched every year into British markets. Some are a great success and some are a great failure; most new products fall somewhere in between. Throughout the book there will be an analysis of some of the failures and they all illustrate one thing. The instigators ignored one of the five basic tenets of marketing which was discussed in the first chapter, and whose deficiencies are measurable. The '5 R' test. (*Right* Product, *Right* Production, *Right* Time, *Right* Price, *Right* Position.)

CAUTIONARY TALE 2

Four different companies launched a cellular telephone that required a local 'call point' (could not be used anywhere) and which could not receive incoming calls. All failed – total estimated costs are £546m. Why?

1 Market research showed that 62 per cent of telephone calls are inbound. This meant that users would have to completely forgo that facility. Unbiased market research indicated that less than 2 per cent of potential users would buy a system that was 'send only', and would only work within a few hundred metres of a call point. In spite of this, millions of pounds were needlessly invested in the systems, the support, recruiting staff, call point sites, advertising etc.

2 Users could pay slightly more for a truly mobile telephone with none of the restrictions on calls or on locality. They found that the phone was a positive contributor to business efficiency and therefore justified the expense. A call-only phone allowed the users to keep in touch with the customers, but would not allow the customers to phone them, thereby precluding 62 per cent of total telephone traffic.

COMMENT

The above companies fail the 5 R tests on the following:

*1 The **Right Product** fails because competitors could provide a full service for marginal extra cost and at much higher efficiency. Instigators were very silly to have ignored their own market research.*

*2 **Right Time** fails because the product was too late. If launched say five years earlier it would have been an advance over the roadside telephone box (most of which were vandalised). This would have led to better communications at that time, and this strategy would have led to an upgrade pathway with added value to a full send/receive system at a later date. It could be argued that **Right Positioning** could also be involved if the product had been marketed at much lower cost and allowing upgrade to a full send-receive service at higher price.*

WHY DO YOU NEED A NEW PRODUCT SCHEME?

As you are already developing new products and services you may think you are happy with your present set-up. Consider this:

1 How many product/services launched in the last two years have started making profits within budget?
2 When you launched new products/services did you find new markets not predicted for it?
3 How often do you say 'if only we had done ... with this product/service'?
4 How much involvement do your customers have with your new product/service?
5 How many existing products/services would you say have a competitive edge?
6 How badly has the recession reduced your customers' orders?
7 What percentage of gross profit comes from products under two years old?
8 Who is your biggest competitor and are you losing ground?
9 How many failed products have you had in the last five years?
10 What will be the product/service portfolio in five years' time? How big will be the company?

If some of the answers posed above look decidedly dusty then read on, the New Product Scheme can help you.

WHAT IS A NEW PRODUCT?

SUCCESS STORY

A new product or service can be new to the market or can be an existing product in a new market area. For example, an inventor designed a hand-held, electronic wind-flow meter for yachtsmen which he sold with some success. He took the same idea and marketed it for the monitoring of gas flows to houses, resulting in a product that was more accurate than existing gas flow meters, 30 per cent of the size and could be digitally interrogated for automated billing. He sold 150,000 units as his first order!

It may be helpful to consider a project as a new product or a collection of new products or services. In the example below, the Trident missile system is a complex 'project' which requires 'many new components and services' to make it happen. Exactly the same applies to a new product which requires a complex set of interactions to take place before the new product can exist in its entirety. Hence a Vanguard submarine system could be thought of as a new product and each of the substituent components as parts to the whole product.

In this text a product is defined as a complex interaction of parties to produce an item or service. A project is the process whereby workers, materials and machinery are made to interact to produce some or all of the components in a product. Confusingly, a project may spawn a number of different products as its output and, conversely, a product may only be able to exist when the outputs of a number of projects come together. The hand-held wind-flow meter was a product, which was a project taken from drawing board to sales. The gas meter contained some of the components of the hand-held unit and the new project was to incorporate them into a gas meter, test and market it, resulting in a completely new product.

A recent National Audit Office report on the Trident missile project blamed various different ministries for the £800m cost overrun of the project. The major error was caused by the Ministry of Defence and is blamed on management breakdown. For example a huge 'ship lift' for the Vanguard class submarine was completed two and half years late and at three times the original price. In all, there were 110 different projects and the Audit Office report criticises the fact that there was no overall single authority to monitor constant design changes which resulted in contractors asking for extra time and money to complete the work.

The first problem is to decide when a product becomes a project and vice versa. The product in this case is the Vanguard class submarine, which required important facilities without which it could not function. In fact it is easy to argue that without the support facilities it was not a product. However, the failure in this case was the inability of a single team to take over and manage the complete product. Consequently, 110 projects which related to the Vanguard class submarines were completed by different teams, with different briefs, timescales, budgets and reporting structures. The net extra cost to the taxpayer was £800m which could and should have been spent on more important and agreed items.

The problems with both local and national government products is that they cost a great deal of money, and there is a natural tendency to allocate responsibility to a large committee whose composition constantly changes. In fact this is generally a recipe for disaster. Ideally there is need for a small tightly focused team to take overall responsibility for the control of the 'product' and then to hive off the control of individual component projects to a project manager who reports directly to the core team. This is at complete variance with the workings of the civil and local government service and needs to be examined closely. If a private company, however large, had a three times cost overrun, and two and half times the completion time, heads would be rolling from the chairman downwards. This is simply because the board of directors of the company is ultimately responsible to their shareholders. The same structure is urgently needed in the public service.

A series of projects may come together to create a 'product'. It is often helpful to ask simple questions about the nature of the project and what effects and benefits it will have. In any event, if the project or product is customer orientated, then there is no reason why the same tenets with regard to products cannot be applied to projects.

If the following question is posed: 'What does this product (project) deliver in the way of customer benefits?' some of the answers will indicate what the product is and how it needs to be managed.

BARE ESSENTIALS OF A NEW PRODUCT SCHEME

Simply, the NPS is merely a checklist of actions and interactions that should be implemented to ensure that an idea is rapidly taken from idea to product, meeting the needs of the 5 R criteria. It aids the decision-making process by providing, at each stage, sufficient information for a clear decision to be taken. Life, regrettably, is never as simple as that!

In practice the NPS needs to be accepted in the same way as quality control, ingrained into the company psyche from the chairman downwards, and turned into a way of life. To return to the orchestra analogy in Chapter 1, the NPS is like the score that the conductor uses to ensure that the right musicians come in at the right time. The workforce, none the less, still needs to be able to hum the tune.

A NPS needs to be as unbureaucratic as possible, but at the same time be able to provide resources (workers, machines, time and money) to progress the potential product. The NPS is designed to make life easier for the developing company and to ensure that it progresses as fast and as smoothly as possible. It also assembles information which considerably aids the decision-making process. The NPS also needs to be a form of social compact, whereby innovators and innovations are given the chance to have a fair hearing, and to ensure that each is given the same unbiased assessment; also that the company (or external organisation) has the same standards of measurement for all potential new products or services.

It is best to establish a number of 'gates' or milestone stages where review decisions are made. Five usually are sufficient, but more complex products may need more. Some may need less. To use a Monopoly analogy, 'when you pass GO you collect £200'.

Commitment

The innovation team will be working long hours to progress the product and its members are probably spending much time, even when at home, thinking or working on the project. If the team completes a series of agreed actions on passing the 'gate', it needs to be assured that the promised commitment by the company, for example, in terms of increased funding, extra staff etc., is forthcoming. By the same token, the company needs to be assured that the time and money being spent on the product is well spent, and that the standards to which it has subscribed are being maintained. Probably of equal importance is the knowledge that the scant company resources are being directed in the best possible way so that the products most likely to succeed are being targeted. It cannot be overstressed, that the 'us and them' situation created by the product team, and the judge and jury system, should not stop the full interflow of information between the two sides. Especially in large companies, senior managers and directors should be kept informed of both the up and down sides of a particular project, and it is most important that they should be consulted on a regular basis if they are able to contribute. Note that such a contribution should be exactly that, a contribution, and not a surrender of the position to a senior manager or director, effectively allowing him to take over the project.

The two-way street

At each gate or milestone, the new project is assessed against a common company 'standard' and this is a sort of contract. The company will agree to provide money for further work, additional manpower or resources, once a gate is reached and to allow the project to progress to the next phase. The actual contract is simple: 'If you pass the assessment at Gate X, then you will be allowed to progress to Gate Y and therefore you are entitled to the resources which you listed as a condition to passing Gate X'. If the company standard is imposed by an external source (bank, merchant bank, venture capitalist) then the review gate becomes essentially a stage payment. Essentially the same rules apply.

Flexibility

The major problems with NPSs is that often they are implemented far too rigidly. For example, at one company, a new product was produced, and inevitably it had a number of variants (i.e. essentially the same product packaged with a different (customer) name on the box). It was insisted that each iteration was treated as a new product. This was a gross waste of time and money and frankly was very bad management, because it acted as a demotivator for the workforce.

What was needed was a 'part number change'. This simple procedure, (ISO 9000/BS5750) allows an existing product to change its packaging (and hence part number) to meet customer requirements. This aspect should be handled by the product management, in conjunction with the sales and technical sales teams, subject to the strictest commercial tests to ensure the profitability and longevity of the variant.

Salespeople naturally want to please their customers by offering a unique product, even if the uniqueness only amounts to the customer's name on the box. Such offers should be strictly controlled against the commercial costs of doing the changes, and measured against the commercial costs of not doing them (e.g. not gaining the business). Part number changes should therefore be kept to a minimum. This procedure can easily be accommodated by the last 'gate' of the scheme.

NEW PRODUCT SCHEME FOR SMALL BUSINESSES

A NPS needs to be intelligently thought out, and may vary from product to product in the same company. However, it needs to have a common template so that the important milestone stages or gates take into account items which in themselves do not amount to much, but which can act as 'showstoppers' if overlooked. Examples are things like patents, trademarks, health and safety, and government and EC/World legislation. Small, medium and large companies alike fall foul of such problems, but small companies are more likely to miss such regulations simply because they do not have the resources to understand or catalogue such needs. The scheme provides regular checks on such problems. However, the use of some external company such as patent agent, trademark agent, trade association or consultant can make up for the lack of in-house expertise. Many trade associations can help with specific legislation which affects their members, and specially when this is in overseas markets. Other sources can be the Department of Trade and Industry, Chambers of Commerce and special interest groups.

We shall consider a couple of example schemes, but please bear in mind that this is a flexible and adaptable scheme and not a 'painting by numbers exercise'. The important thing is that the company adapts the ideas in the scheme to suits its needs. Pragmatically, it is more important that such a scheme is established and run rigidly for a completely new product than say a follow-on product. Even so, follow-on products also suffer problems, simply because the experienced team members tend to go onto other things, passing the control to newer personel who do not have the experience to fall back on. If anything, the scheme should act as a blueprint from design to roll out.

For smaller companies, the scheme may appear to be daunting and the paperwork unnecessary. However, if you need to borrow money to finance the production of the new product, you will find that the scheme will help you in many ways which are not readily apparent. Smaller companies usually know their business very well but have major problems in sharing that knowledge with third parties such as banks and venture capital organisations. Normally the trend is to provide some sort of business plan and accounts to the external money supply and then undergo a whole series of meetings to clarify the arrangements. The third party is seeking to understand the business (and its managers) to help it make an informed investment decision.

In fact, the smaller company may wish to view the bank manager or the venture capital team in the same sort of way, as larger companies will have a New Products Committee, which at the end of the day has to take the same decision as the bank (Stop, Go or Hold). If the basics of the NPS are adopted by smaller companies they will be reporting far more than just a simple business plan and accounts, so that the decision takers (internal managers or directors and external funding sources) will understand far more about the business. They will be more ready to take a decision because the information will have been provided in a professional way, without prompting, and will have important details of market research, production issues, competitors' activity, customer feedback, and customer testing will have been supplied. In fact there should not be any reason why banks or venture capitalists should not use a modified scheme to fund stage payments, in the same sort of way that in large companies the New Products Committee would do. At the same time the NPS will impose a discipline on smaller companies, which should prevent some of the problems caused by elements of the product or market being overlooked. Many large building projects are financed in exactly this way.

The scheme revolves around input and outputs, and is basically no more than common sense. It does however allow for iterative loops and for customer inputs to allow modifications and design changes. It also provides a series of 'checklists' for the less experienced product developer so that important items are not overlooked or considered.

Gate decisions

Clear decision taking is needed in many stages of the scheme. One of the best aspects to a gate decision is that a decision is taken. Generally this is a major advantage to a project, as the timing of the decision will be known because the formal 'gate review' will have been planned. This means that loss of time due to vacillation will be avoided, which is of benefit to both the project and the company. It may be that the decision is to stop the project because of a problem. In such an instance the team is released so that they can devote their efforts to other products and projects. The further delay in such a decision means further loss of time, money and manpower.

Decision

In many of the stages of a scheme there is clear decision taking needed and this may be Go, Stop, Recycle or Hold. Note that the fourth category, Hold, may in certain instances be needed. The project may be considered to have progressed satisfactorily but is put on hold due to some external situation. This could be lack of plant capacity, waiting for a market driver to catch up, changes in statutory regulations etc. In any event, it is a clear signal by the company that the project is of a good standard but that the resources which were to be devoted to it are being switched to other projects until such time as external factors are seen to be favourable for its continued progress. There are some very important points here. The launching of a product too early, achieves very little. The holding of the product at a gate and allowing a rival product greater resources are part of basic good management.

Go

This means that the idea or product is deemed to have met the agreed criteria laid down by the New Products Committee, and that they agree to the extra money, resources, etc. to advance the product to its next review stage.

Stop

Killing a product may seem tough but if the designers of the 'call-only portable telephone' had done so, they would have saved their respective companies some £546m of losses.

Recycle

Recycling of the product may be needed if changes in the marketplace dictate it, or simply if a component or raw material becomes unavailable so that a redesign may be needed. Such recycling is a necessary part of any products development, as customer inputs need incorporating into the design and possible retesting before the project advances to the next phase.

Hold

In the Hold category a product may have been developed and be waiting for the market to catch up. There may be a key need for this product to be driven by another product, or technology which was not sufficiently developed in the market. For example, in CD ROM technology, a manufacturer of a digital sound system had developed a board which provided both the sound element and the interface to the CD ROM drive. Their market research suggested that they could not market their product to CD

ROM makers and they needed to wait until the CD ROM drives became a commodity item below $100. They therefore marketed their sound system and 'waited in the wings' for the volumes to rise on CD ROM drives and their prices to fall. When the trigger point was reached they launched their combined card and are at the moment the market leader in sound cards because their product combines the two tasks better, and at lower cost than their competitors. Also it requires less space within the computer, occupying one expansion slot rather than two. [In this case the product would have been held at Gate 5 – prior to launch.]

Inputs

Some of the inputs need to be unbiased. For example, consumer reaction needs to be very carefully monitored and failure to do so can be very misleading. There is always a temptation to save money by doing the tests 'in house'. In many instances this is OK, but in others unfair weightings result, which means that over-optimistic results cloud the judgement of the scheme. In many instances where a failed product has been subjected to a post mortem it will be found that customer enthusiasm is reported. Criticism is suppressed. This is unfair to everybody as the product will fail Right Product or Right Position test if it is not right for the customer. Some customers may have the 'early adopter' mentality. They may derive satisfaction from being the first in their chosen field to have embraced a new innovation or technology. They will therefore become enthusiastic about a new development and may paint a rosy picture that would not be the same for other customers in the same market. If salespeople are asked to choose trial sites, they are often their 'favourite' customers, with whom they will have developed a long and close relationship. In order not to strain the relationship, the customer may give a more favourable report than say a less involved customer. It is therefore important that a range of customers is chosen, and that the follow-up to their reactions is done by staff who can be frank with the customer on the basis of 'please be objective, and if you think that the product has shortcomings, please say so'. If necessary, statistical sampling may need to be involved, and this is the responsibility of marketing to provide. Technical support teams can often get valuable market feedback by talking to junior members of the customer's staff, rather than to more senior members. The junior members tend to be more forthright, especially if they have been needed to use the product or to install it. In any event, if the input is biased, the result may well be the unfair devotion of resources to a project which, in the end, will fail. This clearly is a situation which should not be allowed to happen. In practice, almost every company will bias some of its findings one way or another. It is up to the team to take a balanced view on this which is why at least one member can often serve the team and company best if he is external, at least, to the immediate group.

CHECKS AND BALANCES

Small companies tend to be much faster to market than large ones, given that they are unlikely to have the same deep pockets and massive resources. This is because they are able to take decisions quickly and often are far closer to their customers, because each member of a small company has to perform more than one job function. The object of the NPS is to introduce the 'small company mentality' so that small focused groups develop new products quickly and cost-effectively and are not hampered by long 'chains of commands' and long delays while decisions are taken. In larger companies , the scheme should help with the decision-taking process, because agreed actions at a milestone or gate result in the decision to proceed being given against previously laid down standards. The team leader must be allowed to argue his position that 'at Gate X it was agreed that if we met the following criteria, we would be allowed to do ... and to have n extra staff ... etc.'.

Part of the small company mentality is that team members are flexible in their job titles. Hence, if the sales and marketing representative on the team is on holiday, there should be no difficulty if the production or R&D representative fields customer questions. In larger companies such crossing over of job titles is often frowned upon, 'because it causes difficulties'. Flexible jobs means better customer interaction, shorter reporting chains, and much better understanding of both customer and internal issues.

This means that large companies have to 'bite the bullet', and accept that they must implicitly trust the development team to make decisions and press on with developing the project. This does not mean an open chequebook but it does mean that the company enters into a contract, in that, if certain agreed criteria are met, then the project is entitled to ask for more money, funding, resources, staff etc.

THE HUMAN MIX

In a NPS, there needs to be a number of key players. Call them 'team leaders' or whatever, the job functions can be briefly summarised:

- The **enabler** who gets things done cuts red tape and barges through inaction and lethargy. Enablers tend to badger the other members and the New Product Committee.
- The **gatekeeper** is the arbiter who ensures fair play and keeps other players to the rules.
- The **devil's advocate** who keeps the team's feet on the ground and plays 'what if ...'. Devil's advocates look for problems.
- The **product champion** (often the inventor or instigator) will brook no delay and may not see fault in his baby. May not be a large commitee man. May have a blinkered approach. Is likely to lead the team in the early phase.

These four are the core of the team. The product champion and the enabler may actually change places as the team leader as time goes on. This process is a natural one, as often the innovators will not enjoy the minutiae of production, packaging or budgeting, and hence are better at being creative. Handing the reins to an able manager who understands and can manage these functions makes good sense. It is, from the human perspective, very important that due communication of the changes in team leadership are managed. It should be widely publicised within the company when changes take place, and they should be positively managed, to the effect that the product champion is handing control to the production manager as the project moves forward, so that he can be released to do further work on the next project or product etc.

The gatekeeper needs to be as independent as possible, and often this suits an outside (say retired) person, who has the necessary technical and managerial skills to provide an unbiased and unemotional referee. The team needs to manage itself with the minimum of interference from outside, unless it is requested from the team itself. The gatekeeper can also provide a balance to a youthful and enthusiastic team, with experience garnered from years of success and failure of past projects, that otherwise would not be readily available in the core team.

The devil's advocate can be internal or external to the company. If internal (often from finance), he needs to be able to grasp both the technical and commercial detail in order to play his role. He will ideally be able to create alternative scenario type models, which will aid the thinking of the team and possibly provide some additional design features that can make the product more flexible, have wider appeal, or be able to adapt to changing markets etc. He needs also to have some market and competitor awareness and may need secondary input from marketing or sales. The devil's advocate needs to be asking questions about who will buy the product or service, who will use it, and why (or why not).

Larger team

Co-opted team members

At each stage there needs to be a series of co-opted team members. In the early stages, the team will be largely of R&D and marketing members. Later on the move will be toward R&D and production and finally toward production and sales. Co-opted members will have many other functions to perform within the company, so their valuable time should be best used. Often it is better to get a junior member of a department to act as representative on a team, with him briefing his senior colleague who can provide important inputs when necessary. In small companies such activities are natural because colleagues tend to communicate as part of everyday activity, calling on expertise only when necessary. In larger companies with many sites, such expertise is often at the other end of the country, making the system harder to work.

At each stage there needs to be a member from each department in the company involved in a watching brief. When the Scheme is outlined in detail, it will be seen that there is a series of inputs, from almost all disciplines within the company. As time goes on the loads may go up or down on the departments, as the product develops from the back of an envelope to a product in a warehouse ready for sale. Watching briefs are important so that future resource requirements can be understood by all departments. Equally as important is that watching briefs tend to provide important feedback to each department and this benefits the project. Departments tend to be more co-operative when they know what is going on.

With most companies it is important that directors and senior managers are involved, but not in the core team. Their strengths are needed in the running of the company as it is, and they should not be distracted by one product or project unless it is large. Even so, they must not be allowed on to the core team, unless they are able to devote unconditionally the time allocation required. For example, the production director of the company should not be on the core team, as he will have continual and often unpredictable demands on his time, which would dilute his effectiveness on the core team and slow the development process. There is a tendency for directors to impose their will and experience on the team, which is actually counter-productive, and can result in bias, which is not helpful.

Each team member, permanent or temporary, must be provided with a simple brief, and must have this imposed on him by the gatekeeper – directors included! Co-opted members should be given the same terms of reference by the gatekeeper as other members, so that their function is clearly defined, not so much for their own use, but so that other members understand why they have been co-opted and what there relevant skills are. On one team I had a complaint from senior management that there were enough engineers anyway when a software engineer was added. I explained that he had no idea what a hammer was for, and that he was heavily into bits and bytes, which was very necessary at that stage!

A note on teams

Many companies are teamed to death. New products need to be led by the core members and need to co-opt a whole variety of different skills to advance the project. These can be summarised for a product which is a physical entity. If the product is a service, or is finance based, then production, production engineering, production packaging will be irrelevant. However, those functions may well be replaced by actuaries, finance controller, health and safety officers and compliance officer etc.

A typical full team

A typical full team will comprise people from the following functions. Such a team would be involved in the middle stages typically between Gates 3 and 5.

- R&D staff
- Development staff
- Finance
- Marketing
- Market research
- Production to productionise the product
- Production engineering to build the plant (if needed)
- Sales to provide input from the customer base
- Production packaging

- Quality control
- Compliance (in certain industries).

One essential feature of any team activity is that the teams must be action led and must not involve extensive team meetings (i.e. talkshops) which take members away from productive work. It is also very important that team members understand their role within the team, and that their contribution is valued from their expertise in a particular area. There is a tendency with some teams to question the decisions of team members, which is only right and proper, but this must not be to the exclusion of their role. In one team the author remembers the production representative continually questioning the marketing department sales forecast which was deemed to be far too high. After launch, it was on the low side, and the team was let down by the production department which failed to trust the sales forecast and had failed to put into place contingency plans to cope with rapidly enlarged volumes. Trust is an important part of any team building exercise, and it is important that each team member is regarded as having equal value, and equal input into the final product. Teams should also be allowed to co-opt members onto the team for a particular phase of a project. For example, there is no point in having a point-of-sale packaging specialist in the core team the whole time, but his expertise will be needed at a certain stage while the product packaging is designed and productionised.

Experts tend to be in demand within companies, so that their managers jealously guard their time. It is important that managers are aware of the importance of their role within both the product and the future success of the company. Wise enablers tend to keep such managers well informed of the product's development, so that when the expert is needed as a co-opted member, he is available at the right time.

From a morale point of view it is often very effective to have a small key team, which will manage the project, and a larger team to do individual parts of the work. It is often good with smaller companies to explain to the entire workforce what the team is doing, why and with what results. It is also important to stress that like a football team, the composition will change over time as the project requires new players and skills, and that there is no shame in a player being dropped as his contribution is finished.

Full teams should meet infrequently, but before a major stage or 'gate' and at any time when full input from all functions is needed. Each member will need to work with a variety of members from different disciplines and there should be a relaxed working relationship with all of them. Very ambitious managers tend to be a hindrance to teams as they bulldoze their thinking into the team's thinking, and tend to be event led rather than product led.

Construction of the teams

Most companies can provide a variety of different personalities from the same department. It is essential that a balance of persons is chosen, as five different department heads, each with strong views, is not a recipe for a smooth-running team.

Balance

It is essential that there are some bright sparks, but also some 'plodders' who will work their way through a project, delivering the goods, but without rocking the boat. Heavily dominant personalities should be avoided, as should inter-office rivalry, as this will profoundly influence the operation of the team, and ultimately the fortunes of the company. The gatekeeper may play an important role in this respect, specially if he is older, wise and knows his colleagues. He needs to select a core team which can work together, and there needs to be a balance between the go-getting attitude of the product champion and the negative thinking of the devil's advocate.

Human nature

The author remembers one team where the R&D representative would always talk down the idea of changing the design of the product in any way. A junior member of the sales team took him out to see a customer who, quite rightly pointed out the shortcomings of the design, and the R&D representative obtained a different perspective on his 'baby'. In order to manage the changes to the design, all that was necessary was to introduce a 'customer idea', which the R&D representative would shoot down at the time, but then 'agree to' in the following days. In his case there was a natural reluctance to agree to something which required change. Such change needed to be thought through, and once this had been done then he would agree to the change and its implementation. Good teams understand the strengths and weakness of their colleagues and are able to manage them, which is why they are good teams.

A human element exists in any such project. Any design change is often seen to be a criticism of the original designer. In fact it is an improvement. This improvement needs to be 'sold' in exactly the same way as a salesperson will sell a product to a sceptical buyer. In many instances, what is needed is to get the designer to put himself in the position of a potential buyer, or user, and to look at his 'baby' from that perspective.

THE 'MODIFICATION' STEP

A staggering array of 'convenience' inventions are produced by individuals who get fed up with using a product that is causing some inconvenience and whose idea is to modify the product in some way to make it easier to use. The vast majority of so-called new products are actually just a series of small improvements on a previous product. For example, in the computer industry the first dot matrix printers used a 5 X 7 matrix, and had a low pin pressure. As time went on the matrix went to 9 X 7, 12 X 9, 18 X 12 and now 24 X 18 dots to create the same character. Any 'new product' in the industry is just a performance improvement, or a cheaper model caused by changes in electronics or the order size, resulting in economies of scale.

For example, the waxed cardboard carton for milk, fruit juices etc. has been on the market for decades. Much of the product does not end up in the right place because the opening of the wretched things has been so difficult, and the subsequent pouring operation has always had an element of chance. The inclusion of a small plastic hinge spout eliminates both the problems with the waxed carton. No doubt invented by somebody who had had enough of milk down their clothes. In this instance what is so surprising is the length of time for the innovation to be marketed. However, the inclusion of a plastic hinged spout, introduces another problem, which is the effective sealing of the container, which is sold as being 'long life'. The successful launch of such a product means that a number of issues with regard to sealing, health and safety, EC regulations have to be understood, researched and solved.

Be aware however that their are often several routes to the same solution. A Japanese inventor produced a musical lavatory seat, which played a merry tune when sat upon, so indicating that the lavatory was in use. A lock would have had the same effect!

RESPONSIBILITY

The team should be given the responsibility to manage the project, and to allocate resources, including spending money on outside help if this is deemed necessary. In smaller companies which lack the resources of larger companies, outside help is often critical in order to obtain information which may be vital to the product. Few companies have their own market research departments and so would commission external surveys. Most companies will have sales teams and would claim to understand their marketplace. However, the employment of a consultant with specific market knowledge may be vital at the early stages of the project because such knowledge may profoundly influence the design and shape of the product. Later on, market research and customer testing will increase the knowledge base of the company.

Devolving responsibility

Some company managers and directors dislike devolving responsibility over money matters. However, it is a prime matter of responsibility. If you are happy to delegate the company's future to new products and to the team put in place, you cannot interfere and not give them the right to spend money. Many senior managers and directors have a real problem in trusting their juniors to be responsible. They express utter surprise when returning from two weeks' holiday that the company is still functioning and has not burnt to the ground. These same people have to learn to trust their junior colleagues, as the new products that a company produces are essentially the future of the company. If the idea is to be turned into cash, you have to trust those to whom you have delegated the job. The process of setting out a budget, relative to the stage or gate, and then letting the team manage it is essential to morale. If the standards imposed at the start of the scheme are correct, then such responsibility can be devolved without the manager or director losing any sleep.

One recent team was obviously put into place to develop new products but also to act as a fall guy if things went wrong. This is clearly unfair and smacks of buck passing. Frankly most team members will smell a rat if they are given supposed powers to manage a project and then find that they have no power. They may plan a project up to the next gate, and then find that an outside director will veto part of the plan. If the board of directors has sanctioned the team to do a job, a single director must not put himself in a position to change or stall a detailed plan. What he should do is to try to guide the thinking of the team down a different route. In doing so, he will suddenly become intimately acquainted with a lot of detail, which will in turn alter his original perspective, and if the team has done the job well they will have his respect and his support. A good salesperson will tell you that often the most vociferous objections, if successfully handled, will result in a solid and supportive buyer. The same applies with projects.

Learning how to act as a team

Many team building consultants will tell you that it is important that teams are built and taught to work together. Probably the best teams are informal gatherings which naturally click together. Rumour has it that Watson and Crick, whose concept of the double DNA helix has played a large part in the understanding of molecular genetics, spent as much time in the pub as the lab! If the pub is the best place for teams to meet then so be it.

The bottom line with any company be it small or large, is for the trust in a project to be passed to those chosen to run it. In some ways, modern management systems can be a disadvantage as well as an advantage. Two hundred years ago if there was a problem on a far off shore, the Admiralty despatched a frigate, and the captain sorted out the problem. A year later the Admiralty was appraised of the result. Today, with instant communications, the captain of a modern frigate is not allowed even to arm his weapon systems without permission from on high. It is very important that the responsibility is devolved to those whose job it is to manage the project and equally it is also important that those involved in running a team feel comfortable discussing the project with senior managers and directors, and it will be very important that a 'feedback loop' is established, so that the management of the company feel confident that the project is under control. Inevitably there will be problems and setbacks. It is good practice for them to be sensitively discussed with the relevant parties.

CASE STUDY

The British Government wanted to rehouse the British Library in a building large enough to house all the works in the English language, and on a scale rivalling that of the US Congress. It earmarked the sum of £118m in 1978, with completion of the library planned for 1985.

By 1994 the building was still not open or being used and the costs had escalated to £450m. No opening is in sight.

Problems include water ingress into the basement areas, failure of the shelving systems to work, incorrect wiring of the electrical circuits, and lack of capacity for the future.

The British Library fails the **Right Product** test because clearly it cannot accommodate more than the existing works in the English language, and there is no capacity for future works.

It also fails the **Right Product** test because the storage of books requires clean and dry conditions. Water ingress into the storage areas is a major design flaw and should have been researched and means found to prevent the problem at the design stage. Apart from water, fire is the other major fear in what is the most important collection of English language books in the world. Again, in the design stage proper effort should have been made to ensure that the wiring was correct both in the design and its implementation.

The mechanical shelf racking system, should have been checked and double checked before the orders were placed. In practice there were problems with the shelves buckling under the weight of the books, and rusting due to the improper treatment of the metal. Any competent specifying engineer could and should have spotted these errors.

A team of independent consultants found that overall control of the project was weak and the project had gone on for so long, that later managers were inheriting mistakes from their predecessors; mistakes that had been under-emphasised deliberately. There was a complete lack of control both overall and at the remedial stages. What was needed was a small team of highly motivated people, whose job was to live with the project, and to ensure that all the designers and contractors did their respective jobs correctly. Nothing in the library project was new, there were no new technologies involved, so that this 'one off new product' could and should have been delivered in budget and on time.

Handling failure

There is also the important point of what happens if a team decides that it cannot continue because one of the 5 R criteria cannot be met. The obvious conclusion is that the project is a failure, and therefore the team responsible is also a failure. In fact look at it from another perspective. The project was a success in that a key driver was found to be lacking and had the project been allowed to continue it would have used up resources, manpower, time and money, which could have been reallocated to other more worthy projects. If the NPS is properly implemented companywide, such a withdrawal will be seen in its correct light, with the best interests of the company at heart. The team should be regarded as heroes not villains.

Analysing success

Almost without exception any successful major project, if analysed, will have a small core team who will drive the project. Most major projects which fail, go over budget or deliver product years late, have large committees, lack of goals and purpose, and often have very badly defined responsibilities. Small teams take upon themselves the pride and responsibility of making the project a success, partly because their reputation is at stake. Large committees are anonymous, so that the blame for failure can be diluted. Parkinson's law may be a work of humour. It is also very true.

Trust is a senior management problem. Either you are prepared to trust your staff and delegate the work or not. If not, then you had better think of another way to develop new products!

SUCCESS STORY

A senior Japanese company director was asked how he viewed his workforce. His reply was that his workforce was a collection of experts who worked together to produce a result. He cited the case of the lathe operator who could machine a part to one thousandth of a millimetre. This man could not write a business plan, nor could he plan a production campaign. Yet without him, the company could not function. He was an expert in using his machine, and should be regarded as an expert in just the same way as the inventor or the accountant.

With such an outlook, it is not hard to understand why the Japanese are pre-eminent in trusting their employees to produce new products.

THE BUSINESS PLAN

At each stage of the Scheme reference will be made to a business plan. In the early stages, the items need to be brief, but as the product and the costs increase, the business plan needs to take increasing hold as the main driver of the scheme, in that input and output need to be understood and the size and scale of the business opportunity implemented in the business plan. The plan itself may need to be subdivided if the product can be produced for several different markets.

The business plan should be a live document, and should grow organically from the 'back of the envelope calculations' at the start, to a full-blown business plan at Gate 5 with roll out costs, competitor analysis, and likely competitor reactions after launch. With modern computers it should not be too difficult to agree a common style of plan, using a commercial computer spreadsheet programme which can form the basis for future projects to report in a common fashion. As spreadsheets can be easily inter-linked, individual modules for a project can be bolted on and the whole unit passed from the project team to the finance department when the product goes live, so that budget forecasts can be painlessly integrated into the company budgets.

Each project is unique. It must be allowed to report in a common style so that members outside the project are quickly able to digest the information and should be presented in a style with which they are familiar. This is just as important with internal assessors as for external assessors (bankers etc.). There can clearly be a case for bankers to have a common format so that each reporting project can report in the same style. This makes the assimilation of the information much easier for the assessors.

The business plan can also be used as a mapping exercise, used to focus the 'downstream' thought processes, specially for the R&D teams, whose choice of design may need to be altered to make the product produceable in economic quantity, or within a time or price constraint. The business plan should involve all the core team and almost all the bit part players, as they will have to contribute to the numbers which go to make the model. It should not be seen as the 'property' of the finance or marketing departments; it should be seen as the product blueprint. In the earlier stages many assumptions will be needed to allow the business plan to function. As time goes on these assumptions will need to be tested, and replaced or altered. Computer and financial modelling is only as good as the data which is fed into it.

One company, in a new product and new market area, assumed that its consumable offtake would be 5 units per year, even though market research in similar markets indicated that 10–15 units was appropriate. In fact they quickly ran out of production capacity, which meant that their Right Production element was sadly wrong. The plant they had built was badly undersized and required the rapid building of a second plant, resulting in considerable sales losses due to lack of capacity. In fact, if they had forecast properly, trusted their market research better, and had beta tested, the results would have indicated that their plant was undersized and corrective action could have been taken much earlier.

JUDGE AND JURY

There are two sides to the table. On the one hand we have the potential new product with its team of supporters, who are competing with other teams for the company's time, money and resources. On the other side we have the company officers; directors, partners, senior managers or even external forces like bank, or venture capital operation. Their perspective is due diligence to hand out and manage the company's resources to make the best use of the resources and to ensure the continued prosperity of the business. They will have to sit in judgement, and they are as important as the teams on the other side of the desk. There needs to be a balance of views from different disciplines, and above all there needs to be experience, specially of the pitfalls along the way. There is a natural tendency to the 'us and them' situation which could be encapsulated by the idea that the team wants the financial backing and the judges won't let them have it.

In fact, that is not the case at all. The judges do want to give the team the money with the certain knowledge that the investment will produce a 500 per cent return and provide a cash cow for the next 20 years. However probity suggests that a little caution is needed. In fact both are on the same side. Their ultimate goal is to produce products which are better than those of their rivals, and in so doing ensure the continued prosperity of the company. In the recent recession many companies have had to shrink in size simply to survive. If you look at the effect of the recession on a particular industry you will find that a few companies buck the trend. Those that do have either been very lucky, or more likely they have bucked the trend by having new products, or have existing products in new markets which have increased their prosperity.

The judge and jury need to be formed into a New Products Committee which should be as formal as the company. Some may just be a collection of senior individuals who meet informally as and when required. Other companies may need to formalise things. What is important is that they are seen to be impartial, and that they have certain ground rules which must be obeyed. It may be an option to include on such committees retired colleagues, who can bring a wealth of industry knowledge and experience, but who are emotionally removed from the fray. The New Products Committee does not have to be remote from its team members on the opposite side, but it does need to define its standards and remit if necessary. More help will come from the scheme itself, but at the end of the day each company is different, and needs to establish its own standards and publish them if there are lots of contenders for the Scheme.

In the Scheme a marking system can be used, so that in a particular phase, a product can be marked out of 100 as a composite score from a multiplicity of facets which have been graded. For example, the product may be required to have passed all safety tests (score rating 5) but may have scored only 3 out 5 for customer enthusiasm. This can be helpful if a number of potential contenders are competing for a limited set of resources. However, it is important that the New Products Committee has agreed on the important criteria for the company, and how to mark them. Some categories will include criteria which 'Must pass' while others will be optional on the score. For example, it may be a criterion that a new product must show at least three discernible new user benefits (score = 3). However some products may be able to show five or six new user benefits. They should be allowed to score all of them. The scoring system should be published so that anyone approaching the committee can score the product for itself.

Smaller companies may not need this complexity, and so the NPC can decide for itself how it will act as judge and jury. However there may even be small companies where the judge and jury find themselves involved in the team. The NPS can still work as long as there is an impartial referee. Most product teams self-score their project at each gate, before approaching the committee, so a small company can do the same. In their case the NPS will be of considerable benefit in providing a checklist of actions which, if overlooked could result in a 'showstopper'.

3

THE NEW PRODUCTS SCHEME

CAUTIONARY TALE 3

A consumer electronics company launched a still video camera. Sales were less than 10 per cent of those projected. This camera was designed to take direct pictures using a video chip rather than film, and then produce a picture either on a television screen, or a 'hard copy' from a video printer.

COMMENT

The company failed for the following reasons:

*1 **Right Time** conditions were too early for the state of the market. Users were not used to viewing 'photographs' on a TV set.*

*2 **Right Position** conditions were wrong. Subsequently the product was aimed at niche commercial applications and is a success.*

*3 **Right Price** conditions were wrong – consumers would not pay £1000 for a camera with inferior performance to a normal photographic camera with a price tag £25–250.*

If the product had been properly beta tested in different market sectors, the costly mistakes would have been avoided, allowing a natural growth into the 'electronic picture' market at the right time.

Alternatively, if the devil's advocate, whose role was depicted in Chapter 2, had played more on the cost/performance ratio of the product, he may have initiated some consumer research which would have led to its sale as a niche product from the start, and saving million of pounds in promotional costs in the wrong market.

GENERAL

What must be clearly understood is that different companies have different products, with different timescales, and marketplaces, and various customer expectations. No two companies will be using exactly the same New Product Scheme, as they will have their own ideas of how to implement it. This may well be influenced by the size and type of company and their past success rates. New Product Schemes are not a panacea, but rather should increase the hit rate of successful new products.

Each scheme needs to be tailored to the company; for example, a life assurance company may have a completely different perspective on a new product than, say, a pet food maker, or a company which makes heavy road rollers. Also, one company with different subsidiaries, may need different versions running in different locations.

The basic Scheme has a number of defined review stages, which can be expanded or contracted dependent on the company, its products or services, and its management style. The understanding of the Scheme requires that all eventualities are considered. How they are handled is a matter for the New Products Committee, acting as the judge and jury, to decide. At each stage, there needs to be a series of sanity checks, namely that the market has not changed, or if it has changed, that the product has been altered with it, or will not be affected by the change. Important features such as changes in raw material supply, changes in legislation over health, changes in the financial climates (pensions, life assurance, bank accounts etc.) need to be monitored regularly, and at each review stage. The assessors need to be satisfied that the changes are being monitored, understood, and product redesign taking place if necessary. (This may be the crucial step between success and failure.)

It is normal to consider a five-stage system which can be broadly summarised as:

Pre-stage 1 **Sanity check ... is this idea worth any consideration as a potential new product?**

Stage 1 **The original idea ... Outline business plan**

Gate 1 **The product looks feasible ... marketable ... produceable ... is potentially profitable ... etc.**

Stage 2 **Padding out the detail ... write more detailed business plan. Produce prototype**

What is the market? ... What is the competition? ... How is it better? ... Can it be produced?

What investment needed? ... New plant? ... What do customers think? ... Any showstoppers?

Gate 2   The product is a potential long-term revenue producer and is worthy of further investigation

Stage 3   Detailed design of product and analysis of the product for markets, patents, competitors, production, samples to customers. Customer alpha test phase. SWOT analysis.

Gate 3   The product will produce volume and profitable business. Business plan is OK. Customer's alpha test favourable

Stage 4   Detailed analysis of alpha test. Is the product right? ... How can it be improved? Can it be made more efficiently/less expensively? Does it meet customer needs? Can it be made in budget? How has competition changed? Any law changes? Product can be produced at costs similar to business plan. Customer research reaction favourable

Gate 4   Product is ready with high degree of success rating. Beta test samples in field. Business plan still needs minor changes only. Looking good

Stage 5   Beta test samples working well. Customer comment good, any adverse comment is being addressed, and improvements are researched and have been productionised. Training underway. Sales channels prepared. No serious competitive threat. BS5750 underway.

Gate 5   The product is ready for sale and may have variant forms. Sales and distribution are ready and advertising and marketing communications are on-line. The product is as good or better than predicted in the business plan, and the make costs are as good as or better than budget. There are no obvious new competitive threats.

Launch

Post   In light of experience, change products due to user vari-
               ance. Work to further reduce production costs

Pyramid system

The Scheme itself will resemble a pyramid system. Pre-stage 1 there
should be, ideally, quite a number of 'potential new ideas' which should
be presented to the judge and jury. Some will pass onto the next stage
which is a preliminary review, and will qualify for some time and effort
to be spent in qualifying the ideas. As later stages or gates are reached,
some projects will get canned for a whole variety of reasons. This shows
that the scheme is working as it should be; weeding out the weaker candi-
dates. Some ideas may still be good ideas, but be put on hold for some
reason, for example a lack of resources or production capacity, too early
for the market etc. What passes into the later stages should be products
with a high degree of potential success given all the constraints of manpower, production, market etc. The author knows of one new product that
was developed as a 'stopgap product' until there was greater production
capacity, when it would be replaced by a newer product still. It proved so
successful that its successor was never built. It is impossible to speculate
as to what might have happened to the company's fortunes if they had
waited for the increase in production capacity, and had launched the successor without a stopgap. However, full marks must go to the team for
understanding that the opportunity was 'NOW' and that a stopgap product
was needed to retain market share.

So, the Scheme will start with a large number of possibles then numbers will reduce quite quickly so that the resources are concentrated on the
'most likely to succeed' candidate(s). The scheme when in operation for
a time, will have produced a number of good ideas, some of which have
failed, some of which are heading towards being new products, and possibly some that are on hold, waiting for one of the Right conditions to be
fulfilled before further work is done. It may well be that in some companies, ideas that cannot make new products can be recycled to improve
existing products and extend their useful life.

Implementation of the Scheme

It will be seen from the above that for the average product, a five-stage
development cycle is enough. However, complex technical products may

need more stages than this, specially if quality feedback from the alpha and beta test stages are analysed, and the product is redesigned.

This may need further alpha and beta test stages before the product is market right, and so more stages may be needed. Experience in the marketplace will allow the New Products Committee to establish the 'rules of engagement' with regard to repeated alpha and beta tests, which are often necessary in some products. From this they can set up the appropriate number of useful gate reviews.

Freezing the specification

An important part of New Products Development is knowing when to stop. There is a tendency for all parties either to offer new features, or for sales and marketing to demand new features, which results in a continuing series of α and β test forms. The technical specification needs to be frozen, and such extras added to the next version. This gives the production department a clear product to learn to make and sell. In most instances such minor improvements have little impact on the market attractiveness of the product but have major delaying effects on productionisation and launch. If several β tests are needed, further gate reviews may be deemed to be necessary. This tends to apply to 'one-off projects' rather than products which are produced in mass volume. Much of the gate review will concern budget and recostings, which are entirely necessary.

Moving the goalposts

In many Audit Commission and Commons Select Committee proceedings, many of the cost overruns are blamed on changes in the original specification of the product or project, resulting in more work being required by the contractors or subcontractors than was tendered for. This is a clear indication of major problems in two areas.

First, the scoping of the product or project in the first place. If the product was wrongly specified at the start, then clearly there is a problem. Second, is the willingness to move specifications and not to freeze the specification and build to it. In the motor car industry there is an expression to 'sign off'. This means that a part, a product or a project is designed and specified and 'signed off' as being completed and approved. Any person who put their signature to a sign off, is also placing their future career prospects on the line. This clearly is the right way to encourage responsibility from the employees, and to ensure the rapid development of a new product which may contain thousands of discrete new parts. Perhaps in government contracts there should be a much higher degree of signing off, so that the taxpayer gets a better thought-out product, at the right price and on time.

Legal, statutory, market regulations

Some products may be legislation sensitive. For example, fiscal products may come and go because of changes in government legislation, EC rules or other directives. Such problems can be potential showstoppers, so that at each gate there may be an analysis of threats, of which legislation may be a part. The removal of a component by lack of supply, legislation, toxicity or other problems must be looked at and handled sensibly. The ground rules should establish if the product can be made and work the same with a substitute. If not, then the system must establish how such a supply failure will alter the product, and how a fasttrack reappraisal of the product can be done using the scheme. It must be realised that the redesign of the product may reduce its market attractiveness in some markets which may have a major impact on the whole business plan.

As an example, if a plasticiser is withdrawn for safety reasons, will this profoundly affect the rubber components in a product? If the answer is yes, then new alpha and beta tests may be needed. It certainly will not profoundly alter the business plan, the market size, or the business opportunity.

Early stages

This sanity check should be capable of being run in conjunction with many others. There may be many bright ideas floating around the company. This brief check should sort the wheat from the chaff, and will allow some projects to be held in limbo if the timing is not right, or the plant capacity is wrong, or as in the case of financial products, the regulations are not right. The sanity check prior to Stage 1 should still be documented to a very limited degree. What may be absolutely unworkable and preposterous one year, may be the basis of a new product next year!

The idea stage and sizing of the potential opportunity

Objective: To look at some of the assumptions and to fill out some broad ideas on market size, who will buy, why, and whether it fits the company's product range, and whether it is makeable. A Japanese steel producer went into producing laptop computers, which had to compete with many other products, produced by computer makers, who had far more industry and commercial experience in that market. The product was a good product, but failed, simply because volumes were not high enough. It is important therefore that a new product can be seen to fit into the company's product portfolio, or if not, the clear routes to market via external sources. At the early stage it would be wrong to kill a good potential project out of hand, but the NPC should be seriously looking for how the company is going to make sales in a completely new (and alien) market sector. Equally the team should be looking for natural alliances or even joint ventures in order to increase their success ratings in a new market sector.

The sizing of the opportunity needs to be by necessity brief and to the point. Wise innovators at this stage talk to their colleagues in different disciplines to get thumbnail sketches of production capability, market sizes etc., so that their initial proposal is as well prepared as possible, given the total lack of resources at this stage. Assessors will be looking for novel ideas and not detail at this stage, and a submission to Gate 1 will enable a limited amount of company time and money to be devoted to filling in a broad outline.

Stage 1 – The sanity check

A product proposal plan is a slightly more sophisticated version of the back of an envelope. It needs to be widely circulated, and needs to be the subject of constructive criticism. Ideally the comments need to come from both in house and from the real world – e.g. customers.

However, a note of caution here. If the product is a result of intellectual property rights, is patentable or similar, then the direct discussion of the idea with a customer could invalidate its subsequent patent application. No hard and fast rules apply, but probably the best bet is to discuss matters with customers in broad terms, 'if we could solve your problem here … etc.' rather than 'if we design this to do that to solve your problem etc.'. In fact, the information you are looking for is the fact that there is a problem, and that if it can be solved, then the company has a product which customers will buy. Most buyers base their buying decision on solving a problem, making their life easier, greater efficiency etc. It is important at this early stage that the potential project maps out why the potential customer would buy. Focus at this stage on the reasons for buying will often influence the subsequent design and the product's positioning. The microcomputer company example in Chapter 4, and its operating system, would have benefited from a very early stage, asking who will buy it and why. (And just as significantly who will not buy and why?)

Market research at this stage does not have to be extensive – merely to scope the scale of the markets, and the obvious competition. In the market research of competitor companies, it is worth using the sales force to 'trawl' the marketplace to find competitors, and specially new entrant products. Market research companies tend to be lagging behind in this area, and often a salesman can talk to a well-informed distributor in the marketplace who has the necessary 'on the street' information that may not be widely known elsewhere. Talking to the editors of trade papers is always another good source of gossip and can also be of great help later on if the product makes the grade, as the editor will feel that in his own small way he helped the product along. Trade paper editors tend to have a lot of vital industry knowledge, which again can be of benefit to smaller companies who are venturing into a new market. Editors tend to be very helpful in many areas, and it costs near to nothing to ask their opinion or advice. They will also have many other contacts, who can be used as sanity checks and are often very happy to do so.

BUSINESS PLAN

The business plan needs to start with a number of basic assumptions and then to grow with the project so that it is being constantly updated and refined, assumptions need to be replaced with firm numbers as time goes on, and as the business plan grows, margin analysis, competitor threats, competitor reactions should be included. If the product is going into more than one market sector, then it is good sense to run separate sections and consolidate them at the end. The activity of a competitive technology in one sector may have no effect at all on the other sectors, so the threats should be quantified as separate undertakings, and then consolidated at the end.

α test

The α test is essential to any project. It tests both the product and the company and corrects important design flaws, marketing mis-assumptions, and indicates from customer feedback the likelihood of customer success. Many good α tests include design ideas and improvement from the customers. Customer 'hand holding' may be necessary with some technical products and will be a vital source of information and insight as to how real customers behave in the real world. The α test should test the pre-production prototype with customers, and get their reaction. It can also provide important pointers as to how the subsequent marketing should take place.

A major Japanese manufacturer of office products built its first smaller office photocopier, and then α tested it and found major problems with the toner/drum assembly, which would normally have been sorted out by the field service force. As this was a completely new market area for them, they realised they had a major problem, as they did not have a field service force at all. They had either to ditch the project, or redesign the machine. They did the latter, and in doing so, produced a product which had the toner/drum assembly in a disposable assembly, so that unlike their competitors, no field maintenance was needed. Each time the toner ran out, the complete assembly was changed. Having pioneered this in the small photocopier market this same idea was used in the emerging laser printer market resulting in their becoming the largest maker of laser printer products in the world, which position they have maintained for the last 13 years.

β test

The β test is designed to test the product as you expect to produce it, and should be a random production sample. It should test everything including packaging, instruction leaflets, instruction manuals, installation procedures, so that it is a test of the product in the field 'without any hand holding'. The β test will also give a wider variety of field conditions and applications and will inevitably flag problems that were not anticipated, simply because the information was not available from customer interaction and the α test.

A car radio manufacturer launched a new product some years ago, to find that in his beta test the product worked well over a whole range of cars except one make where the product would inexplicably fail. On examination of the beta test results, it was found that the one make of car that failed had a faulty wiring loom which resulted in excessive drain on the radio circuit. The inclusion of a simple diode device stopped this at a cost of a few pence, and the product was a success. However, the important point is that a problem in the field, which was not identified (and could not be reasonably identified) by other means, was solved before volume production took place. The actual costs involved were quite small. If the beta test had not identified the problem then the costs would have been much higher, both in terms of damaged radio sets, and in damage to the reputation of the maker. Unfortunately, the maker would have been blamed for a fault which was actually of the car maker's origin.

New Products Committee

Ultimately the assessors will be the decision takers with regard to the company's resources, policy and money supply. They may be company directors, general managers, or they may be external assessors such as bank managers or venture capital teams. It is often quite helpful if there are external assessors, say industry consultants, as they will have a different perspective on the potential new products, from those within a company. Industry consultants often have a lot of industry knowledge and hence can assess products like a surrogate customer. Non-executive directors are not usually suitable unless they have direct industry experience.

PRELIMINARY ASSESSMENT TO STAGE 1

This is inevitably a very difficult stage. In the course of a year there must be literally hundreds of ideas which could become products that will be dismissed out of hand, simply because of basic problems with design, production, regulation or funding. The object of the scheme is to encourage the promotion of new ideas and to grant them a fair hearing, and essentially to weed the good idea from those which are unworkable for whatever reason. It is very important that a rejected idea is not totally discarded and, with modifications, is recycled. It is also important that the rejected inventor is encouraged to try again and not alienated by the process.

One of the major problems with a general New Products Scheme is that it never fits the needs of any company without a degree of modification. This is totally accepted, and it is unrealistic to expect the design of a new tin opener to share a lot in common with a new insurance policy. However, the concepts of the five gate reviews, of market testing, of customer feedback, or competitor review, is common to all products, and is probably quite adequate for most purposes. Small companies will not need to be so rigorous in its application as the lines of communication are a lot shorter, hence decision taking is much easier. One of the major strengths of a small company is the speed at which it can react and it would be wrong to make anything less flexible than it needs to be. However, in smaller companies there is inevitably less material available for acting as sounding boards, as most employees are very near to the business both literally and emotionally. In such situations it may need the unbiased views of independent persons who can be co-opted from chambers of commerce, trade associations, technical colleges.

Small companies and external funds

While small companies may resent the extra methods required, they will find that the extra work does pay dividends, as it aids thinking. If external funding is needed, it provides a comprehensive assessment of the product, far beyond what most external funding sources are used to or would normally receive.

Put yourself in the position of a bank manager who has received literally hundreds of requests for loans to fund small companies. If he receives not only the business plan, but also competitor analysis, market research findings, complete products costings, channel margins etc., this is far more comprehensive than normal. He is likely to view the application more favourably than many of the other requests he gets. Small companies regard financial institutions as bottomless wells of funds. Most presentations to bankers are not well received because the bankers can see the advantages, but can also see the pitfalls. The more comprehensive the presentation, the better the bankers can understand both the product and the company behind it. In the end the bankers are not backing the product, they are backing the sound judgement and business skill of the company. They are more likely to back a company that has presented a well-prepared case and has considered all sorts of additional parameters which will influence the business case.

Potential showstoppers

It is quite fascinating to see product development in action. Recently a product was removed off the launchpad at Stage 5 + simply because it was unsaleable in its form. The reason was simple. It contained carcinogenic material which was unacceptable. No part of the development process had considered whether the materials used were safe. This is why at every stage, there are health and safety, patent, legal and fiscal requirement checks.

EC and government rules change daily, so that it is important to check these issues on a regular basis and the various gate reviews make a convenient point. Surprisingly many products trip up on small items like legal needs. For example, a French company started the import of some of its electrical goods into the North American market, having made them specially to 110 V 60 cycles. However, what they had overlooked was that such products have to have Federal Communications Agency approval to ensure that they do not cause radio, telephone and general interference. They, and their distributors, were prevented from selling them until each item was approved which cost many months in time, and lost a lot of customer goodwill.

Product outline

In the preliminary stages, the outline of the product must include whether it can be made, or whether a new process is going to have to be developed to make it. It is also a good discipline to provide an end user-based price, and then work this back to a 'make' price, in order that the scale of costs are understood. Technical and R&D staff, often have little production knowledge, and hence may grossly underestimate the required sale price. Therefore it is often worth talking to a distributor in the marketplace and pass the proposed end user price by him. Inevitably he will form a view that the price needs to be lower than a competitor's product which has better features, or maybe higher, on the grounds that the proposed new product has features which provide added value. In any event, the establishment of an 'end user' price allows a quick estimate of the 'make' price and hence may indicate volumes, manufacturing techniques, and route to market.

In the preliminary stages, wide consultation will help the project and should allow the inventor to 'feel the waters' to establish enthusiastic partners for the first stages of the project. Ideally, marketing and production should be involved to give the necessary scopes to estimated figures and to provide costings, market sizes etc. However, some service and financial products do not have a production element, so in that instance maybe an industry expert may be needed to provide advice as to the shape and nature of the new product.

Action plans

In the Scheme, at each gate an action plan is called for, so that who does what, when, and for what reason, is implemented immediately on passing the gate review. In some instances the action plan may need to be part of the gate review, as it may affect the company in important manufacturing detail. A gate review which requires the trial running of an existing plant in a modified way to produce a new product clearly has major impact on the nature of the business. Action plans decide who does what, and for what reason. They are also a good way of estimating the time, and hence the cost, of the personnel who are required to deliver the action over a defined timescale.

Action plans tend to get more complicated once external forces are needed. For example, the action plan may be to report complete costings on the replacement of the No. 2 production machine with the latest No. 8a. This is going to involve some very serious discussion with outside parties and may require a lot of work. Some parties may not move as fast as the action plan dictates, so there has to be a certain degree of tolerance between the agreed action and the size of the task. For example, at an early gate there may be a need to establish the size of the world market for a product. Market research may be able to quickly identify US and European demand, but not for other territories. It may be acceptable to factorise the known figures in order to estimate the world market size. Later on, that guesstimate will have to be seriously revisited, as it will be important, not only to estimate the unknown size, but also to identify the players, the competition, the sales channels etc., that would contribute to market intelligence. By that later stage however, there would also be the money and/or staff time to be devoted to a more detailed study.

A small manufacturing company may think it has a new product for a market sector that is unfamiliar. The salesman may be despatched to talk to a medium-size local distributor, and come back with a set of figures which can be scaled up to provide an outline demand forecast. In the early stages this may well be sufficient and acceptable to the NPC. Immediately before launch it will not be so! Action plans will tend to be biased toward certain disciplines according to the stage of the project. In the early stages it will be R&D, marketing and market research. This will move onto development and production, and later still to production and sales. It is important that each representative of the core team is able to cope with the workload, or is able to second help to cope with the load.

Control

The gatekeeper will need to ensure that such loads are manageable and that adequate resources are allocated. Feedback is a vital element in any action plan because an action in one area can have knock-on effects in other areas. For example, a salesman may report back from the field that distribution has reported a 'buying resistance' to a completely unrelated product due to the pack size being too large. It may then be deemed worth considering a smaller pack size so that the resale price falls below a given 'buying resistance limit'. This needs to be considered not only by the sales and marketing department, but also by production and packaging. For example, it may require some research to be conducted as to whether the original observation is fair by asking a selected sample of potential customers. Such observations are the life blood of new products, but also can be time-consuming to trip up the unwary. At the gate the decision may be made to go forward, to wait or to kill the idea.

In the early stages, there are a number of kill or hold recommendations, due simply to the volume of ideas. Successful projects tend to go on quickly in the later stages. However, later gate reviews should be just as rigorous. There may be a tendency to adopt the attitude that 'we have got so far down the line' that this latest setback may not be serious. Beware of such sentiment! To cancel a project at one of its later stages is far less costly in time, money, manpower, and kudos, than to launch a product which fails because of an identified problem. In the case of the call-only mobile telephone the signs were very clear. Unfortunately, those within the project and those with the power and purse strings chose to ignore them. The net cost was £0.5bn.

Interactive discussion

It is important that both team members and the NPC are able to discuss problems which arise in detail. The downsizing or underemphasis of a problem can create major product weakness, which could cause a catastrophe. In the case of the small photocopier α test, a major and apparently insurmountable problem was solved to almost create a new industry. However, there are products that may wait at the earlier gates simply because it is felt that they are too early for a reasonable market, or waiting for another driver in that marketplace to catch up.

There will be awkward cases of inaction due to such comments as 'no demand for the product as far as we can see'. Akio Morita, the Chairman of Sony reported this comment, having made some preliminary prototypes of the world famous Walkman. Exhaustive market research revealed 'no demand' which was not surprising as the product did not exist in the minds of the public. He wisely ignored it. As the results show, the Walkman was a classic marketing triumph of right product at right time. Put through the New Products Scheme it could have died before Gate 1! It is also a very important aspect of the Scheme that directors are not allowed to seriously weight the thinking of the development teams. There are of course exceptions which should be defined thus: 'Directors may override the ideas and aspirations of the team, on the strict understanding that they are funding the entire programme from their own pockets'. This usually concentrates the mind wonderfully! In the case of Morita, the rest is history and his decision to overrule his marketing team was right.

Therefore it is necessary that some intelligent guidelines are laid down and understood.

The concept of the Boston square

This simple 2 x 2 matrix indicates the degree of difficulty in selling products. For example selling a new product in an existing market is far easier than selling a new product in a new market (which is what Sony did). In some cases, the product itself will create a new market.

It is important therefore at the outset to understand that the more difficult the market, the higher the rewards, and also the higher the risks. This must be taken into account in the preliminary stages, and must be taken as a factor which may not be quantifiable at the very early stage. It may be that a new and innovative idea may require to be considered by consumer focus groups at an earlier stage than the scheme would normally require, A strong consumer reaction would obviously provide major support for further investigation and funding. A strongly negative reaction may require either the holding or the killing of the project.

The Boston square is of great help in understanding the relative positioning of products. For example, the company may have three different potential products. A simple product upgrade to an existing product (A), a new product in an existing market (B) and a completely new product in a new market (C). If the Risk versus Reward is plotted for the three different products, this can help with the decision as to what gets funding and what does not.

Risk v. reward

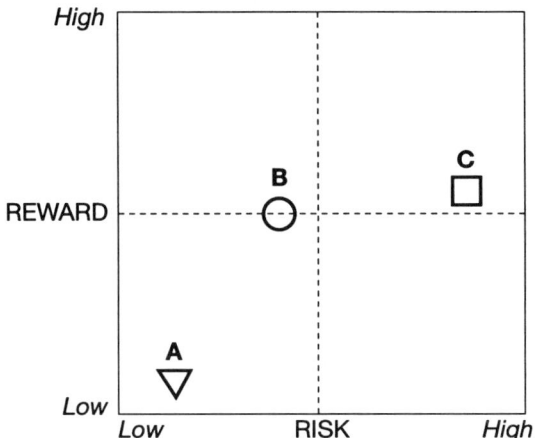

Clearly the exercise indicates that product B has about the same reward factors, without the same risks, as product C.

Interactive situations

During the passage of this book various situations will be detailed in order to demonstrate some of the problems associated with the Scheme and there will be ample opportunity for the individual reader to formulate a range of ideas. At the end there are comments which I hope will be helpful but it is clear that as in life there is no simple clear-cut answer. For group discussion I hope that the fur will fly, as this will be the best way to tease out a whole range of ideas that support the following scenario.

While the actual situation is fictitious, the problems and decisions are exactly the same as would be faced by any person or group involved as the judge and jury. At the end of the description, setting the scene, will be a number of questions. Sample answers will be found in the Appendix. They are by no means the only viable answers!

Your role as reader

You are a director of the company, and you and other directors are reviewing the initial idea and being asked to pass it to Gate 1 of the New Products Scheme.

SITUATION 1

Goldwell Chemical Company is well known for its organics and fine chemical intermediates. Dr Gough, one of its younger and enthusiastic researchers, has found that under certain circumstances, 2 methyl fer-richrome, and certain inorganic metals such as zinc, iridium and aluminium can be made to interact in the presence of light and generate electric voltages. He has constructed a simple cell composed of a glass outer rectangular section tube containing the solution which is gold coloured and one iridium and one zinc electrode. A volume of 120 ml of solution generates a consistent voltage of 0.8 volts and 0.5 amps in a light level of 5 lux and above.

Dr Gough believes that with suitable development this cell will provide the following:

1 Low-voltage–light-induced electricity generation at 10 per cent of current (silicon) prices
2 Medium voltage daytime power generation for air-conditioning etc.
3 Low-cost daytime generation for night battery storage in remote areas
4 Emission-free electricity generation as backup to mains power generation during daylight.

He believes that the product has certain possibilities:

1 Allows Goldwell to sell to third-party 'battery makers' under licence
2 Allows Goldwell to sell the 2 methyl ferrichrome
3 Allows Goldwell to develop and sell its own industrial cells.

A preliminary 'look see' by Andy Rawlish in the marketing department indicates that the provisional pricing of the cell would indeed be about 1/10th of the pricing for silicon 'solar panels' on a per sq. metre basis. World volume for these products is a series of small niche markets, ranging from solar-powered calculators to solar-powered telephones, telemetry, remote sensing and similar. The overall market is put at about £100m per year.

Andy has contacted two relatively large users of silicon solar panels and they have produced a prediction that, as cost is the limiting factor, if the new product is 1/10th the price, then the market will explode – possibly 20 times the current size, giving a potential of £2b. Goldwell's research teams think that the production of the glass containers (in series) and the sealing of them will not produce any major technical problems. There is some preliminary evidence to suggest that a purer grade of iridium may be beneficial to the long-term stability of the cell solution, so that the life of the cell could be as much as ten years. Gough and his team are asking for further resources to:

1 Conduct a better market research report on product, costs and benefits
2 Construct several different prototypes to test variance and performance
3 Employ two researchers on a full-time basis for six months
4 Employ four part-time persons on external contacts with battery makers and electronics manufacturers, and writing up a patent.

Q1 *What questions do you ask at this stage to satisfy yourself of the viability of the proposal?*

Q2 *Subject to satisfactory answers from above would you go/stop/hold? Justify your decision*

SITUATION 2

You are a manager sitting on the New Products Committee. Your advice is being sought on the following problem.

Foster and Small is a company involved in metal alloys and their supply to a wide range of clients for industrial use. Paul Samton, on the sales team, had his company car stolen from outside his house by a joyrider. The car was found and the police informed him that an experienced thief could break into the vehicle in less than two minutes and break the steering lock, hot wire the car and drive it away.

Paul has looked at the very weak aluminium castings used in the steering lock, and has taken the broken sample to the research lab. Don Brallen, head of alloys R&D has taken a brief look and agrees that the lock is very weak. He believes that he can put together an aluminium alloy which is ten times as hard, which would be so strong as to resist the crowbar used to break the existing lock. He and Paul draw up a basic plan to produce an alloy to replace soft aluminium in the steering lock.

Q1 *What information do you think that they should provide at preliminary stage in order to qualify for Stage 1 funding?*

4

STEPS TO A SUCCESSFUL NEW PRODUCT

CAUTIONARY TALE 4

A worldwide microcomputer company developed a new operating system that required considerable cost increases in hardware expenditure, with no definable increases in computer or user performance (at that time).

COMMENT

The product failed because:

1 *It failed the* **Right Product** *test because it did not offer anything major in terms of performance against the existing products and it required major capital expenditure to work at all. It sold less than 8 per cent of the market predicted for it because it had no discernible benefits, added cost to the user, plus the learning of a new command set.*

2 *It failed the* **Right Time** *test because, launched later, it would have met new user criteria, which the older systems could not offer, and without the need for expensive hardware upgrades.*

3 *It also probably failed the* **Right Position** *test, in that it could have been marketed as a 'high performance with no obsolescence' criteria, which all its competitors lacked.*

Objective

A sanity check to ensure that the idea warrants further discussion and investment in time and money.

Checklist

Sanity checks

- Prepare written description of invention or idea and circulate to interested parties
- Describe likely market sectors and segments and relevant sales channels
- Describe competitive pressure from similar products and also different technologies
- Identify customer needs and benefits and any sustainable advantages
- Health and safety issues. Can it be produced safely? Any pollution problems. Regulations/licences?
- Fit with existing company products and services – any conflict?
- Rough idea of costs and resource needs? (To produce better understood analysis)
- Suggested price structure and sales channel
- Identify customer profile and reason for buying. Superior product benefits.

Action plans

Defines who does what, on what timescale and why the action is needed in order to advance the project to the next stage. Enabler ensures that actions are accepted and understood by each individual.

STAGE 1 TO GATE 1 REVIEW

Purpose

Any idea which passes the 'Gate 1 review' is worthy of the company's full attention and will get attention and funding to pursue the advancement of the project to shape up its potential.

Required inputs

- The description of the idea
- Existing or new market potential
- Competition including same technologies and also different technologies which compete for the customer
- Superior customer benefits. Compare and contrast with existing market leader if identified

- Development issues
- Production issues
- Strategic fit with existing products and distribution network (if relevant)
- Approximate costs, revenues, resources
- If a new product, in a new market sector, proposed sales channels or strategic alliance.

Test criteria

Must meet

- Strategic alignment
- Reasonable technical feasibility
- Suitable market size
- Good payback potential
- No health and safety problems
- No legislation problems.

Should meet

- Synergy criteria
- Market attractiveness
- Superior customer benefits
- Willing core team to advance the project.

DECISION

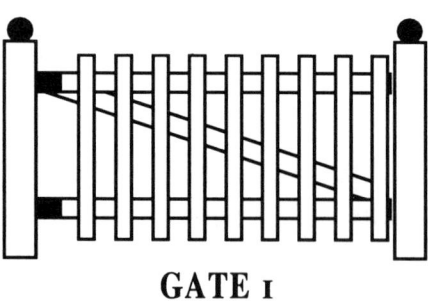

GATE 1

Go forward/Wait/Not viable

If **Go forward**

Output

- **Action plan to Stage 2**

STAGE 2 TO GATE 2 REVIEW

Preliminary investigation

Objective

To establish that there is a ready and viable market opportunity and that the company can offer a differentiated product and make and/or supply it at an acceptable profit margin. That it fits either within an existing product group or within the company's expanding product ranges and markets.

Checklist

Marketing

- Produce a product proposal plan which includes customer base, customer needs, broad product specification, crude pricing structure, with sales forecast, volume and timescales
- Identify and expose real potential customers for the product
- Identify any competitor advantage. Is it sustainable? Can it be made so?
- Write market research plan
- Preliminary business plan in outline form.

Research and development

- First pass technical assessment with feasibility, production, health and safety, patent, legal problems
- Resource requirements for next Stage 3 assuming passing Gate 2 review.

Production and engineering

- Outline of possible raw material/component supply options. Timescales?
- New plant costs, or loading on existing plants, including packaging etc. Timescales to modify or order and commission and test new plant.

Finance

- Maintain watching brief over outline business plan and provide relevant software module.

DECISION

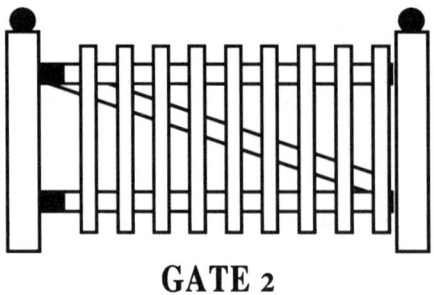

GATE 2

Go forward/Wait/Not viable

If **Go forward**

Output

• **Action plan to Stage 3**

STAGE 3 TO GATE 3

Opportunity review and full product definition

Purpose

This review ensures that the opportunity is worthwhile, can be achieved, technically and commercially within the timescales, and that the company can make available the wider resources required for Stage 3. If the company cannot make available wider resources, due to other commitments, the project can be put on Hold.

A major 'risk versus reward' assessment should be made before major capital is committed.

Required inputs

• Market plans
• Customer reaction to the idea
• Reassessment of R&D and production capability
• Health and safety issues are OK
• Preliminary finance plan
• Outline of resources needed
• Short review of market changes since last gate review.

Test criteria

Must meet

- Strategic alignment
- Reasonable likelihood of success
- Suitable market size
- Feasible business plan
- No health and safety problems
- Good production and producability potential.

Should meet

- Synergy criteria
- Positive customer response
- Superior customer benefits
- Ability to sustain product on a long-term basis from competition.

Checklist

Marketing

- Provide business plan in some detail
- Outline product specification(s)
- Using prototypes user-led market research with feedback comment to technical teams
- Provide clear statements on health and safety, patent/copyright, and any legal issues
- Complete competitor analysis
- Milestone development plan
- Relevant technical service requirements.

Research and development

- Develop product to the stage where the performance characteristics are clearly demonstrated
- Development stages plan with milestones
- Possible need for technical appraisal of competitors' products.

Production and engineering

- Complete summary of manpower, raw materials, component sources, plant and packaging

- Summary of new plant costs and conversion work on existing plant with timescales
- Impact on existing production on other products if modifications to plant are needed.

Finance

- Provide preliminary finance plan with profit and loss, cash flow and capital account
- Become the prime mover in establishing the business plan.

DECISION

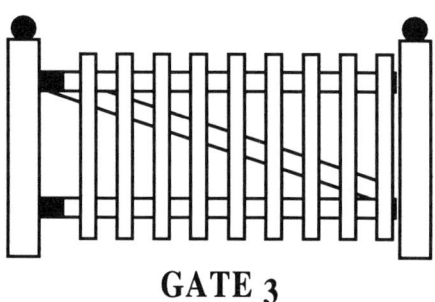

GATE 3

Go forward/Wait/Not viable

If **Go forward (otherwise hold –)**

Output

- **Action plan to Stage 4**

STAGE 4 TO GATE 4

Full development of product

Objective

To be able to develop the product fully so that all the required features can be tested and technically checked by real customers, and the product should be in a state where productionisation can take place. Customer-led interaction should allow the product to be redesigned in light of full customer reaction, if necessary, and this should be subject to further iterative testing if needed. It is likely that BS5750/ISO9000 procedures would commence at this stage.

Test criteria

Must meet

- Strategic alignment
- Excellent likelihood of success
- Good market size
- Robust business plan
- No Health & Safety problems
- Good production and production ability
- No patent, legal, trademark or market problems
- Product is as good or better than predicted.

Should meet

- Synergy criteria
- Excellent customer response
- Sustainable customer benefits
- Ability to differentiate product on a long term basis from competition.

Checklist

Marketing

- Carry out customer sampling on the α test programme, with full feedback
- Comprehensive survey of competitor products, prices, price attrition and markets
- Full business plan, marketing plan, and production plan
- Update of sales and volume forecasts
- Write initial product data specification and data sheet
- Implement and design a test plan, with feedback loops, and statistical forecasting
- Implement technical service needs and train
- Likely competitor reactions, with computer modelling if needed
- Design and implement packaging, instruction leaflets, technical manuals, installation guides etc.

Research and development

- Review with production feedback from a test and modify product in light of test
- Provide a reliable product specification. Freeze specification once customer reaction is rechecked
- Provide a technical assessment of the competitor products.

Production and engineering

- Provide complete summary of production including actual and potential bottlenecks. Look at possibility of faster than expected growth, and how this would be handled
- Packaging and warehouse requirements and developments if needed
- Write out capital order(s) for new plant or equipment as required
- Plan for production of modified α test product, and scale up to β test numbers.

Finance

- Firm up previous finance plan with better figures
- Work hard on updating the business plan, replacing estimates with reliable figures.

DECISION

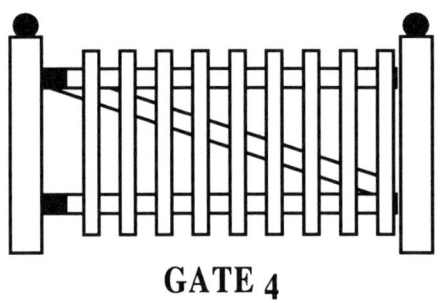

GATE 4

Go forward/Wait/Not viable

If **Go forward**

Output

- **Action plan to Stage 5**

STAGE 5 TO GATE 5

Pre-launch

Objective

To be able to produce the product totally reliably, or assemble the products in house to the standards of quality laid down, and expected

by customers and to deliver the volume required with no showstoppers. The product will be a major revenue generator and will contribute to both overheads and profits for a considerable timescale. The product can be produced within budget, and is delivering the expected customer benefits predicted for it and quality is as good or better than its rivals.

Test criteria

Must meet
- Excellent likelihood of success
- Good market size
- Excellent long term profitability
- Robust business plan
- No Health & Safety problems
- Robust production, no quality or make problems
- No patent, legal, trademark or market showstoppers
- Pricing is as predicted. No major changes in market pricing. No price wars among competitors.

Should meet
- Robust sales forecast. Presales activity
- Excellent customer response
- Product offers sustainable benefits. No similar competitor launches
- β test results good. Any field problems rectified
- Ability to differentiate product on a long term basis from competition.

Checklist

Marketing

- Design and identify sites for β test programme, with full feedback
- Prepare customers, distribution channels, for launch
- Implement full sales literature, prices, and shows/exhibitions/adverts where relevant
- Set prices and pricing policy
- Carry out sales force and distributor training
- Establish technical service function with technical developments where relevant
- Work with sales to establish sales plan, sales targets and timescales.

Research and development

- Develop β test sampling and assessment procedures, with product

variance sampling and feedback to production
- Technical training for support and sales staff
- Work to produce zero defect quality and establish BS5750 specifications and start write-up.

Production and engineering

- Despatch β test product. Be confident of producing product to same specification as β test product, in volume and to budget
- Finish training staff in production and complete BS5750 write-up
- Devise and train staff in quality control procedures
- Write out procedures to handle different part numbers, and arrange for rapid customer response as production starts.

Finance

- Firm up previous finance plan with better figures (again)
- Continue business plan updates and development. Encourage sales forecasting and feedback.

DECISION

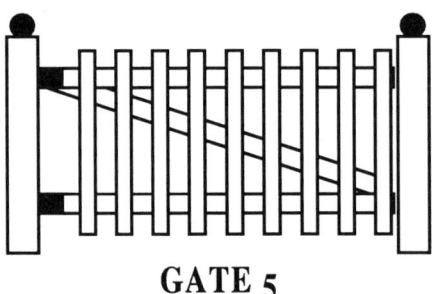

GATE 5

Go forward/Wait/Not viable

If **Go forward**

STAGE 6

Output

- **Action plan to Launch and Full Production**

LAUNCH

Purpose

The product will be launched and will be a success, only subject to a final look at any statutory, legal, patent or other regulations which may affect the viability of the product.

Required inputs

- Sales plan and sales forecast
- Any problems arising from β test have been fully addressed and solved
- Competitor activity, pricing is acceptable and within predictions
- Adequate stocks can be generated to meet sales forecast
- Proof of robust and quality manufacture
- PR, advertising ready for action
- All sales support activities ready to go. Training complete
- Final look at all relevant legislation, patents, copyrights, trademarks, national and international rules.

Test criteria

Must meet
- Marketing communications and sales force activity in progress
- Robust manufacture with no major problems on quantity
- Excellent product quality, which is as good or better than the competition
- Pricing is as predicted and within customer acceptance limits
- Good profitability profile
- No competitor launches which would threaten the product's viability
- Product is being made at costs equal to or better than predicted.

Should meet
- Sales forecast close to initial production make
- Customer documentation is correct and up to date
- Post sales technical and quality assessments in place
- Production/technical assessments as to cost reductions
- Part number changes in place to meet trade customers' own-brand needs
- Market feedback with regard to competitor reaction, pricing, competitor distribution reaction
- Corrections in sales forecasting in light of launch
- Follow-up PR and advertising to increase sales impact after initial launch.

5

STEPS TO A SUCCESSFUL NEW SERVICE

CAUTIONARY TALE 5

A major high street bank launched a new bank account for 'higher paid executives' the 'only account you will ever need'. It included gold card, free banking if in credit, free foreign exchange dealings, etc. Within six months most people attracted to the account had left it. Why?

The account could not offer standing order payments. The gold card, which acted both as debit card and ATM card could not be used as a cheque guarantee card. The result was that the chequebook was virtually worthless, as no trader would accept the cheques. A separate account for standing orders and a cheque guarantee card was necessary, in order for the bank to provide the semblance of normal banking service.

COMMENT

1 *The account failed the **Right Product** test, simply because it did not offer even the basics of a normal bank account, chequebook and standing orders.*

2 *The account failed the **Right Position** criteria, simply because it is clear that the bank wanted to attract the higher income earners. It failed in the concept of the 'only account you will ever need', and alienated a whole sector of the market in the higher income bracket.*

Objective

A sanity check to ensure that the idea warrants further discussion and investment in time and money.

Checklist

Sanity checks

- Prepare written description of idea and circulate to interested parties
- Describe likely market sectors and segments and relevant sales channels
- Describe competitive pressure from similar service products
- Identify customer needs and benefits and any market opportunities/failings
- Legal issues. Regulations/licences. Warranty problems. Statutory requirements. Industry regulations?
- Fit with existing company services – any conflict?
- Rough idea of costs and resource needs? (To produce better understood analysis)
- Suggested price structure and sales channels
- Identify customer profile and reason for buying service. Superior service benefits.

Action plans

Defines who does what, on what timescale and why the action is needed in order to advance the project to the next stage. Enabler ensures that actions are accepted and understood by each individual

STAGE 1 TO GATE 1 REVIEW

Purpose

Any idea which passes the Gate 1 review is worthy of the company's full attention and will get attention and funding to pursue the advancement of the project to shape up its potential.

Required inputs

- The description of the idea
- Existing or new market potential
- Competition: what exists, and their strengths and weaknesses. Failings in existing service offerings
- Superior customer benefits. Compare and contrast with existing market leader if identified

- Development issues. What is needed, on what timescales. What influences the development?
- Strategic fit with existing services and services network (if relevant)
- Approximate costs, revenues, resources
- If a new service, in a new market sector, proposed sales channels, or strategic alliance.

Test criteria

Must meet

- Strategic alignment
- Reasonable feasibility
- Suitable market size
- Good payback potential
- No health and safety problems
- No legislation problems

Should meet

- Synergy criteria
- Market attractiveness
- Superior customer benefits
- Willing core team to advance the project
- Ability to be market tested in a limited way.

DECISION

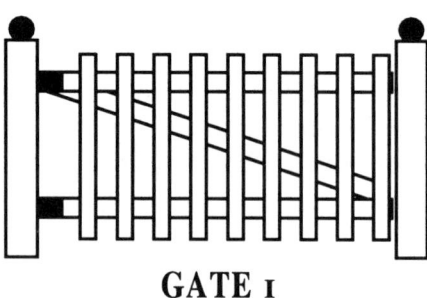

GATE 1

Go Forward/Wait/Not viable

If **Go forward**

Output

- **Action plan to Stage 2**

STAGE 2 TO GATE 2 REVIEW

Preliminary investigation

Objective

To establish that there is a ready and viable market opportunity and that the company can offer a differentiated service and supply it at an acceptable profit margin. That it fits either within an existing service group or within the company's expanding service ranges and markets. If it is a completely new service and a new market area, and is by definition 'high risk', that all parties agree that the risk versus reward factor is acceptable.

Checklist

Marketing

- Produce a service proposal plan which includes customer base, customer needs, broad service specification, crude pricing structure, with sales forecast, volume and timescales
- Identify and expose real potential customers for the service
- Identify any competitor advantage. Is it sustainable? Can it be made so?
- Write market research plan
- Preliminary business plan in outline form.

Research and development

- First pass technical assessment with feasibility, serviceability, health and safety, patent, legal problems
- Resource requirements for next Stage 3 assuming passing Gate 2 review.

Servicing

- Outline of possible human resources, and training. Timescales?

- Costs of literature, publicity, commission structures etc.

DECISION

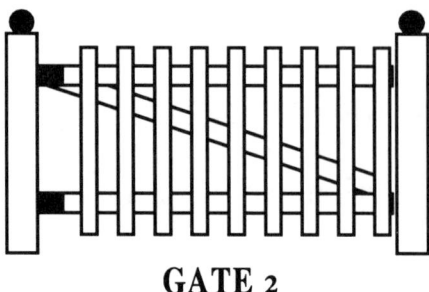

GATE 2

Go forward/Wait/Not viable

If **Go forward**

Output

- **Action plan to Stage 3**

STAGE 3 TO GATE 3

Opportunity review

Purpose

This review ensures that the opportunity is worthwhile, can be achieved, technically and commercially within the timescales, and that the company can make available the wider resources required for Stage 3. If the company cannot make available wider resources due to other commitments, the project can be put on Hold.

Required inputs

- Market plans
- Customer reaction to the idea
- Reassessment of R&D and service capability
- Health and safety issues are OK
- Preliminary finance plan
- Outline of resources needed
- Short review of any market changes since last gate review.

Test criteria

Must meet

- Strategic alignment
- Reasonable likelihood of success
- Suitable market size
- Feasible business plan
- No health and safety problems
- Good ability to provide service to customer satisfaction.

Should meet

- Synergy criteria
- Positive customer response
- Superior customer benefits
- Ability to sustain service on a long-term basis from competition.

DECISION

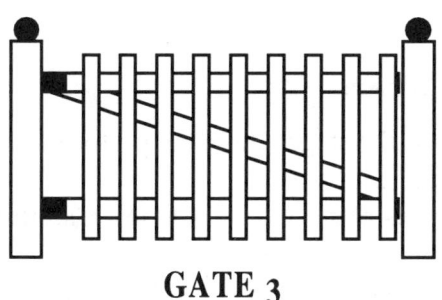

GATE 3

Go forward/Wait/Not viable

If **Go forward** (otherwise hold –)

Output

- **Action plan to Stage 4**

STAGE 4 TO GATE 4

Full-blown definition of service

Objective

To be able to see the service in its final form and to be able to clearly

**assess the risk v. reward before major expenditure. (This is the most
critical phase.)**

Checklist

Marketing

- Provide business plan in some detail
- Outline service specification(s)
- Establish user-led market research with feedback comment to technical
  and R&D teams
- Provide clear statements on health and safety, patent/copyright, and
  any legal issues
- Complete competitor analysis
- Milestone development plan
- Relevant technical service requirements.

Research and development

- Develop service to the stage where the performance characteristics are
  clearly demonstrated
- Development stages plan with milestones. Can this be integrated into
  the existing company structure?
- Possible need for technical appraisal of competitor's services.

Servicing

- Complete summary of manpower, materials, component sources, IT
  needs
- Summary of training and conversion work for existing staff. Training
  plan with timescales
- Impact on existing services.

Finance

- Provide preliminary finance plan with profit and loss, cash flow and
  capital account
- Become the prime mover in establishing the business plan.

DECISION

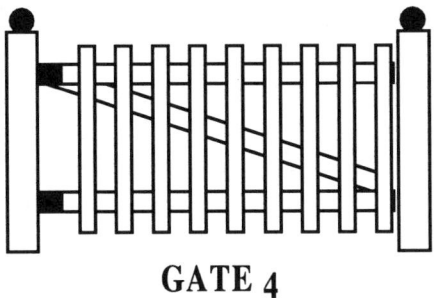

GATE 4

Go forward/Wait/Not viable

If **Go forward**

Output

- **Action plan to Stage 5**

STAGE 5

Purpose

Passing this gate review indicates a strong desire to develop the service fully, so that the service can be fully tested by representative samples of real customers and to gain and monitor field experience so that the service can be reviewed or modified in light of field experience.

FULL DEVELOPMENT OF SERVICE

Objective

To be able to develop the service fully so that all the required features can be tested and technically checked by real customers, and the service should be in a state where service implementation can take place. It is likely that BS5750/ISO9000 procedures would commence at this stage.

Checklist

Marketing

- Carry out customer sampling on the α test programme, with full feedback

- Comprehensive survey of competitor services, prices, price attrition and markets
- Full business plan, marketing plan, and services plan
- Update of sales and volume forecasts
- Write customer service charter and circulate within and external to company
- Implement and design α test plan, with feedback loops, and statistical forecasting
- Implement technical service needs and train
- Likely competitor reactions, with computer modelling if needed
- Design and implement packaging, instruction leaflets, technical manuals, sales guides etc.

Research and development

- Review with customer services feedback from α test and modify service in light of test
- Provide a reliable service specification. Freeze specification
- Provide a technical assessment of the competitor services.

Services

- Provide complete summary of services including actual and potential bottlenecks. Look at possibility of faster than expected growth, and how this would be handled
- Requirement for service centres, regions, and control
- As a result of α test input, redesign for and scale up to β test numbers
- Obtain field force comment on α test. Revise training to prepare for β test.

Finance

- Firm up previous finance plan with better figures
- Work hard on updating the business plan, replacing estimates with reliable figures.

DECISION

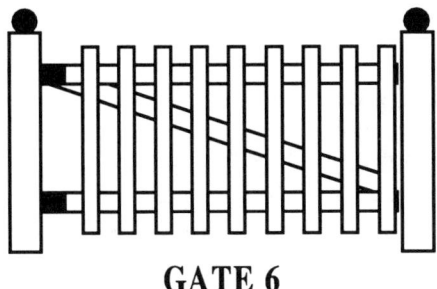

GATE 6

Go forward/Wait/Not viable

If **Go forward**

Output

- **Action plan to Stage 7**

PRE-LAUNCH

Objective

To be able to produce the service totally reliably or assemble the services in house to the standards of quality laid down and expected by customers, and to deliver the volume required with no showstoppers. The service will be a major revenue generator and will contribute to both overheads and profits for a considerable timescale.

Checklist

Marketing

- Design and identify sites for β test programme, with full feedback
- Prepare customers, distribution channels, for launch
- Implement full sales literature, prices, and shows/exhibitions/adverts where relevant
- Set prices and pricing policy
- Carry out sales force and distributor training to agreed external standards where relevant
- Establish technical service function with technical departments where relevant

- Work with sales to establish sales plan, sales targets and timescales.

Research and development

- Develop β test sampling and assessment procedures, with service variance sampling and feedback to services
- Technical training for support and sales staff
- Work to produce zero defect quality and establish BS5750 specifications and start write-up.

Services

- Test β test service. Be confident of producing service to same specification as β test service, in volume and to budget
- Finish training staff in services and complete BS5750 write-up
- Devise and train staff in quality control procedures. Implement random customer satisfaction sampling
- Write out procedures to handle different service variants, and arrange for rapid customer response as service starts.

Finance

- Firm up previous finance plan with better figures (again)
- Continue business plan updates and development. Encourage sales forecasting and feedback.

DECISION

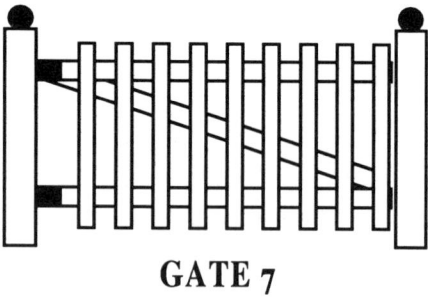

GATE 7

Go forward/Wait/Not viable

If **Go forward**

STAGE 8

Output
- **Action plan to Launch Full Service**

LAUNCH

Purpose

The service will be launched and will be a success

Required inputs

- Sales plan and sales forecast
- Any problems arising from β test have been fully addressed and solved
- Competitor activity checked, pricing is acceptable and within predictions
- Service needs are fully in place
- Service offered fully meets customer expectations and is as good or better than rival offerings
- PR, advertising ready for action
- All sales support activities ready to go. Training complete
- Final look at all relevant legislation, patents, copyrights, trademarks, national and international rules.

Test criteria

Must meet

- Marketing communications and sales force activity in progress
- Robust service with no major problems on quantity or quality
- Excellent service quality, which is as good or better than the competition
- Pricing is as predicted and within customer acceptance limits
- Good profitability profile
- No competitor launches which would threaten the service's viability
- Service cost being made at costs equal to or better than predicted.

Should meet

- Sales forecast close to initial prediction

- Customer documentation is correct and up to date
- Post sales technical and quality assessments in place
- Service/technical assessments as to cost reductions
- Market feedback with regard to competitor reaction, pricing, competitor distribution reaction
- Corrections in sales forecasting in light of launch
- Follow-up PR and advertising to increase sales impact after initial launch.

6

RULES OF ENGAGEMENT:
The Sanity Check

CAUTIONARY TALE 6

A manufacturer introduced a new improved flow valve which cut dramatically certain accidents in hydraulic working. After launch they were swamped with orders and were unable to keep up production, losing out to their main rival. The rival, having had so many product enquiries (which it could not meet), and indications of the new market, in the meantime had essentially copied the design and produced it.

COMMENT

*The maker failed the **Right Production** test. He trailblazed his new product, showed his competitors the new market and then failed to back his product with adequate production, losing market share to his rivals.*

There is an important lesson here. If you produce something, which trailblazes a new market, and fail to support that market, you are pointing the way to your competitors. Publicity and advertising which you initiated, will have raised the expectations of the market. If you cannot supply, and your rival can, then he will benefit directly from you and your activities. You should consider all the options of patents and registered industrial designs as well as demand forecasting, to ensure right production quantities.

GENERAL

Action lists

The pass from the preliminary assessment and sanity check needs to rely on an agreed action list with timescales. Action lists will by necessity involve persons from within the team nucleus and beyond and hence may involve the time of persons engaged in other projects. It is vital that these 'co-opted' persons are properly budgeted for during the gate review.

If, for example, the services of a market researcher are needed for a few days to do some preliminary market sizing, he will have been taken off another project. His boss will need to be kept well informed of what is going on and why the team are asking for the market researcher's time from the NPC, before the gate review. Wise product champions keep department heads fully in the picture, as they could be providing substantial work if their new baby is allowed to grow. Product champions will of course have fully consulted the market research department and attempted to squeeze it dry on any relevant information before the gate review. In any event, a list of actions will be drawn up, and should be agreed either by the core team, or a designated member – often the enabler.

Smaller companies

Smaller companies will not have the luxury of such operations, and they may need to sanction the services of an external company, or possibly employ an outside individual to find out the information. In any event, the action list should be agreed with all relevant parties before the gate review so that if the NPC approves the action, the consequent actions are not a surprise to any of the proposed participants or their line managers. It is important that the costs of such actions are clearly defined and put into a budget.

It is important to encourage a rapid development from the sanity check stage, to the next gate review so that further and more detailed information is set out to understand both the opportunities and the pitfalls, for a balanced decision to be reached.

Conditional advances to next stage

Clearly some details may take weeks or months to collect so it may be important that there are subjective reviews, which are based on:

(a) 'assuming the costs of the new plant are not greater than £x then proceed to gate nn'
(b) 'assuming that the financial regulator agrees that the outline scheme is acceptable'
(c) 'assuming ingredient x is not found to be carcinogenic or dangerous'.

The complex job of obtaining the complete costs of building a new plant may take months to get the estimates and such delay may not be justified. On the other hand, if the costs are widely out from the original guesstimate then the pricing of the finished product may change and adversely affect the product's chances in the market against competition. Hence a guarded 'go forward' statement allows other parts of the project to proceed without adversely affecting the speed to fruition.

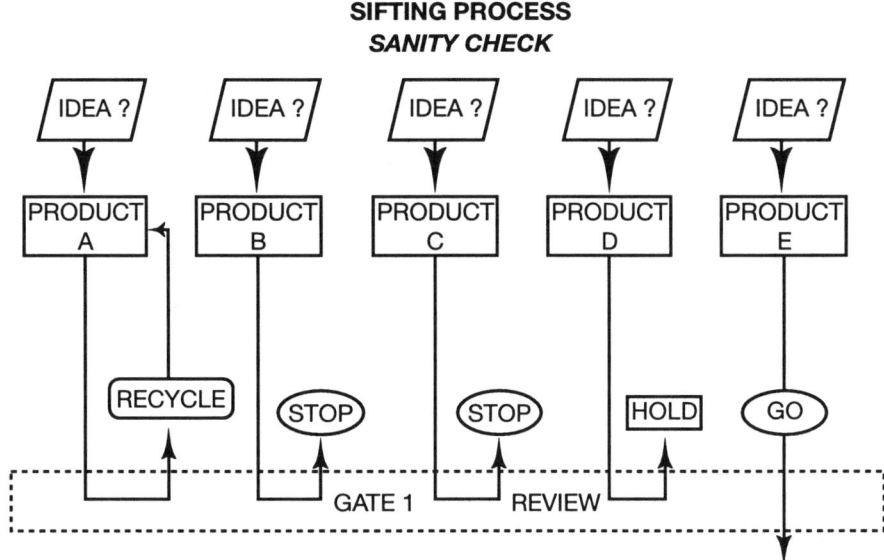

SIFTING PROCESS
SANITY CHECK

Draft business plan

At this stage a draft business plan needs to be written, ideally by marketing or possibly by finance. It needs to be brief but to be structured in such a way as to be expandable as time goes on. Many companies have standard plans, usually based on one of the popular software packages on the market. These should be used as early as possible to predict as many of the unknowns as possible.

Many small companies do not think that a draft business plan is worth it. With respect, a good business plan will convince the most jaded accountant or bank manager and my experience is that the better presented, almost regardless of content, the more likely it will be accepted. A business plan indicates that you have taken into account a whole range of parameters. If written on a microcomputer, it allows a whole range of 'what if' criteria to be entered and calculated.

Product proposal plan

The product proposal plan, should look at different options, and as far as is practical be both market and customer led. From this, one or more 'products' should develop, and it is important not to produce more than necessary. This can then allow a crude costing, feasibility of manufacture, volume and timescales to be made. Often at this stage there may be a number of different potential products, depending on the input and aimed at different markets. At this stage flexibility is the key.

There needs to be clear input from the customer base, bearing in mind that often niche markets are overlooked and niche today may be mainstream tomorrow. The objective with the product proposal plan is to get a high degree of commonality of the components, features etc., without closing too many doors. Later on there will have to be some clear thinking to select the 'product' and to trim down the options.

Customer sampling

It is often a very good exercise to work with some sort of statistical sampling technique to select the customer base, and then to conduct a sample interview, ideally over the telephone to save money.

There may be problems with this in that the company may not be patent protected (as yet), or may wish not to have its identity established, so that it competitors know what it is doing. Some sort of third-party organisation can conduct such interviews, but they do not come cheap.

SITUATION 2

Parry & Brown Ltd have been making garden products since 1959. They specialise in ornamental fruit cages, pergolas, greenhouses and conservatories and they have a good reputation and would describe themselves as being conservative in both product and outlook.

Owing to the recession, Owen Parry, the son of the founder Nick Parry, has asked his workforce for new ideas to expand their product range. Paul Tooting, a young draughtsman, recently visited Holland with his girlfriend and at Leiden saw a new octagonal-shaped pergola in brown PVC. The Dutch company had priced it on the high side and Paul has come back with the idea that Parry & Brown could make a similar product in a variety of sizes and add a new and innovative product line. However, Parry & Brown, have always used wood before for all their products and plastics is a new area for them. Paul has made some initial enquiries and has found that there are several options with regard to supply of the plastic uprights and beams. The Dutch sample used different diameters of uprights and poles, but Paul has sketched some designs which use a standard diameter cross-section, which means reducing the sourcing problems. However, regardless of this, there is also the problem of joining the sections in an attractive way to create the octagon.

Paul can source 150mm diameter PVC tube in brown, ex stock from a supplier in 3, 4 and 6 metre lengths. Paul can also have the same section specially made in thicker PVC which requires the specialist production of an extrusion tool that will cost £12,500 and take three months to make and test.

Paul has assembled a team of enthusiastic junior employees and has obtained permission to make up a prototype, using PVC 150mm tube. They have assembled two sizes of PVC pergola, and general comments are favourable from interested spectators. However, problems have arisen, in that the tubes, having a thin wall, tend to bend when loaded to simulate the weight of plants growing on the pergola. Paul has discussed this with his boss Tony Brown, who has an idea that they may be able to fill the lumen of the tube with a lightweight polyurethane foam that is used in similar applications in the building of tall masts for sailing boats resulting in a much stiffer structure. Paul has the following options:

1 Continue with the same type of PVC tube
2 Try the polyurethane foam route to increase rigidity
3 Pay for a thicker wall sample with the tooling cost and time delays
4 Start again and use wood
5 Abandon the idea
6 Try something else.

Paul needs to spend some time in mapping out what needs to be done to advance the product's case with the senior management.

Q? *What does he need to do?*

SITUATION 3

Anders & Weightell Ltd are involved in a range of packaging for retail sale. In the last two years there have been several consumer complaints about their metal bottle tops cutting users when trying to open the bottle for the first time. In addition, they are losing orders to a competitor.

Paul Mander, their Packaging Production Manager has had an initial 'look see' passed to Stage 1 so that the opportunity can be scoped. In conjunction with engineering, they are looking at replacing the metal screw caps with plastic ones. Customer response is good and the main issues are of experience, capital expense, and timescales. The market research indicates good marketplaces, with expanding requirements, and there are no health issues.

Paul Mander is having problems however in the potential production of plastic screw caps. They have had no experience of plastics injection moulding. They have a number of options:

1 Design product and have it made by a third-party moulder in their name
2 Employ a consultant to advise them
3 Employ an experienced injection moulding manager and start a new department
4 Buy the necessary capital machinery and get on with it!

Preliminary costing suggests that plastic caps cost about 80 per cent of the cost of metal ones to make, from a materials point of view. However, the capital costs are much higher, as the old metal-forming machinery is bought and fully depreciated, whilst new plastics injection moulding machines are expensive on new capital.

Results indicate that plastic caps are going to cost about 5 per cent more to produce at the same profit margins as the metal ones.

Q1 *What questions would you ask with regard to the future cap business at A & W?*
Q2 *What are the options as to the future of the product range?*
Q3 *What would you suggest are the necessary actions if the gate review is passed?*

SITUATION 4

The Capital & Municipal Assurance Company has, for many years, been selling its products via third-party agents and has in recent years suffered strong competition from newer entrants into the market. John Appledore, the Marketing Manager, has capitalised on the strengths of C & M in the property market and has researched and tested a range of products for the house and commercial property markets. The product team has realised that it should also be selling pensions and life assurance to the same customer base and argue that C & M should be proactive in the market.

Appledore is apprehensive about certain financial institutions including banks, building societies and insurance companies, buying up small local estate agents and forming large groups through which they can sell their financial services. Appledore wants 'in on the action', and has got one of his marketing assistants to identify a number of smallish estate agents that could be welded into a nationwide chain. Appledore is making a presentation under the New Products Scheme. You are on the panel of the New Products Committee.

Q1 *What justification should be proposed for his large chain?*
Q2 *What are the strengths and weaknesses of his plan?*
Q3 *Is there any other way to get to the same market and could it be less costly and more profitable?*

SITUATION 5

Polders & Sons sells a range of confectionery products via up-market high street stores, some of their own name, and also in department stores. About 50 per cent of the confections are made at its factory while the other 50 per cent are bought in.

Andrew Brown, who is the grandson of the founding Bent Polders, while travelling in Russia came across a confection which he liked. It was imported and sold very well in the stores. However, the problem is that it is very difficult to get reliable deliveries from Russia. Raw material purchases in Russia make it difficult for the maker to get reliable supplies and hence to deliver consistently. Deliveries by air are very expensive and by sea slow and unreliable. Andrew has scheduled a meeting of various departments and is posing the following ideas:

1 Is the product line worth pursuing?
2 What is the customer reaction to the product given that it has not been advertised?
3 Can the company continue to sell with only sporadic supplies?
4 Could the company license the product and make it in the UK?
5 Failing licensing, can the company produce a similar-tasting product?

The following information should come out of the meeting:

Q1 *What sort of demand forecast should be made?*
Q2 *What is the cost of making the product in the UK – production issues?*
Q3 *How will the product sell if advertised?*
Q4 *Are there competitor products and do they sell well in UK?*
Q5 *How do profit margins compare with bought-in and made in UK?*

7

STAGE 1:
Firming up the Opportunity

CAUTIONARY TALE 7

Recent changes in legislation resulted in a bonanza for pension and life assurance companies to sell pensions to individuals subject to occupational pension schemes, such as doctors, nurses, teachers, local authority workers etc.

A range of products was produced by major companies and was sold to unsuspecting clients, regardless of whether the product was *as good or better* than the occupational schemes. Claims were made to convince potential clients, that were untrue. A recent survey by Peat Marwick McLintock, of over 1000 policies, shows that 4 out of 5 clients were sold products which were inferior to the occupational schemes. The Securities and Investment Board has pronounced that compensation must be made to those policyholders who have, or will, lose out. The amounts are estimated to be in the order of £7bn. An SIB report in October 1994 indicates that compensation is likely to be about £1bn. Their report indicates that in some instances salespeople were clearly trained and briefed by their company to make claims which were overstating the benefits of their product as against occupational schemes. As the practice was so widespread they conclude that it must have been company policy and not the salesperson individually.

COMMENT

Such a result is a disaster for the industry! If the policies had been properly designed and cleared by the SIB, before launch, then this would not have happened.

*The companies therefore fail on **Right Product**, as the products were misrepresented. If they had used a New Products Scheme this would not have happened.*

*In addition, the companies will have very seriously damaged their indivi-
dual reputations and the industry as a whole is in disrepute. Also they will
incur major costs repairing the damage and implementing corrective
action.*

GETTING STARTED

This is one of the most exciting parts of a project. The core team members will have to start their business and personal relationships. They will
have to put in place the necessary work to scope the nature of the potential product, and establish the viability of the potential product.

Business plan

Many small companies do not think that a draft business plan is worth it.
With respect, a good business plan will convince the most jaded accountant or bank manager, and my experience is that the better presented,
regardless of content, the more likely that it will be accepted. A business
plan indicates that you have taken into account a whole range of parameters. If written on a microcomputer it allows a whole range of 'what if'
criteria to be entered and calculated. At this stage it needs to be nothing
more than a simple 'back of the envelope calculation' but the plan can
become the major driver of the Scheme as it will establish the rewards that
will come with a successful product. Assumptions will need to be rife at
this stage. Later on, fact will need to have replaced the estimates. Within
the company, the same outline plan can be used to focus attention on the
product. It often helps if the profits potential is large!

Writing business plans is not easy when you have not done it before.
There are several good books on the subject, and Edward Blackwell's
How to Write a Business Plan (Kogan Page) is typical. There are also various 'macros' that are marketed as 'computer business plans' that use
popular spreadsheets such as Microsoft Excel and Lotus 123 as the basic
program.

Product proposal plan

The product proposal plan should look at different options and as far as is
practical be both market and customer led. From this, one or more 'products' should develop, and it is important not to produce more than is

necessary. This can then allow a crude costing, feasibility of manufacture, volumes and timescales to be made. Often at this stage there may be a number of different potential products, dependent on the input, and aimed at different markets. Flexibility is the key at this stage.

MARKET RESEARCH

Customer input

There needs to be clear input from the customer base, bearing in mind that niche markets are overlooked, and niche today, may be mainstream tomorrow. The objective with the product proposal plan is to get a high degree of commonality of the components, features etc., without closing too many doors. Later on, there will have to be some clear thinking to select the 'product' and to trim down the options. It is often a very good exercise to work with some sort of statistical sampling technique to select the customer base and then to conduct sample interviews, ideally over the telephone, to save money.

Confidentiality

There may be problems with confidentiality. The product may not be patent protected (as yet), or the company may not wish to be identified, lest competitors know what it is doing. Some sort of third-party organisation can conduct such interviews, but they are not cheap. However, that money is often well spent, because it provides a totally unbiased answer. If the idea is received favourably then it is confirmation that the product is 'about right'. If unfavourable, these should be in a rethinking of the idea and the potential product. The message is simple; the better the customer input at this stage, the better the chances of success.

Caveats

An alternative can be to select and train suitable student interviewers from appropriate disciplines and use them to do the interviews anonymously. As they will not have the necessary experience of making telephone appointments, it is often preferable to employ a telesales operation to do that part of the job. Smaller companies tend to be a lot closer to their customers, and so can just 'float ideas' off their customers. Beware however, that you may be revealing something which is patentable. In the case of a service or a proposed new service, asking too many questions may give the game away, at least to the customers. Also beware that there is a tendency to discuss new products in place of the existing product which you supply. This 'downgrading of performance' of your present product, may result in your customer thinking actively about it, and selecting an alternative supplier if you cannot deliver the goods. It is often a good idea to talk to the customer on a 'what if' basis. 'What if we could make the new part stronger and 30 per cent lighter?' (The fact is that you may want to switch from steel to aluminium – but in pitching the question in that way, you get the answer without giving too much away.)

'When you spoke to our sales correspondent last month, you indicated that you were having trouble in getting your Mk 4 Widgets serviced. Have you found someone and how much did it cost?' (If the Mk 4 Widgets are still unserviced, he will tell you in no uncertain terms. If he did get them done, he will, no doubt indicate that it was well in excess of what he thought he should be paying.)

Exposing product opportunities

What is clear at this stage is that the marketing department must expose the product opportunity, and all the actual and potential markets. This requires good market research and needs to be from a variety of sources. Good market research companies can provide tailor-made and standard report-type services, but in the area of new products they are often poorly or totally uninformed. In some industries such as IT, very good informed opinions can be garnered from such bodies as user groups, or special interest groups, who in marketing terms act as the trailblazer for new technologies, and are referred to as 'early adopters'. In many instances they will have used a new innovation to solve a specific (niche) technical problem, which will give important pointers as to how this new innovation will eventually find a larger marketplace.

Usually the existing sales network will have good contacts, and it is a good idea to float 'what if' presentations at internal sales meetings and conferences, as this gains access to a lot of knowledge in a short space of time. Sales forces are fickle animals. They need to be very well prepared, as they tend to evangelise new products, even before they are actually there, and in doing so, can often talk themselves out of a sale. This is specially true in capital goods markets, where a customer may be wanting to place an order in the near future to replace older equipment, but will put the purchase on hold if he knows that a newer product is to be announced.

Wrong assumptions

In one instance, the author was involved in a product being sold for use in the computer industry as a consumable for computer-based printers. The market research team, composed of both internal and external members, looked at hardware costs based over time and found that on a ten-year life span, the hardware had come down in price by a factor of 200 per cent, comparing more or less, like with like. They assumed, wrongly, that consumable pricing followed the same pattern.

In fact, the author, once consulted, was able to point to clear evidence that there was virtually no price change in real terms over the ten-year period, and that the same basic consumable (plastic mouldings etc.) were still in use, even though the newer printers were much lower cost and had better performance, which still used the same format and type of consumable. This made a fundamental change in the selling prices over time and completely changed the shape of the revenue forecasts and the profits in the business plan. Put simply, it made the difference between pass and fail in that marketplace.

A very simple example of this is the electronic calculator. The price of the calculator called the Sinclair Cambridge was launched in the early seventies for £49.99, using small batteries costing less than 40p. Ten years later the same calculator was being sold for less than £5, with the batteries costing 75p.

New markets

There is a common problem when trying to market a new product in a new market, as there is not the wealth of experience to fall back on. Hence it is a valuable exercise to consult both internal sales teams and external customers as much as possible. At a final analysis, specially in a new marketplace, it is a good idea to employ the services of an experienced industry consultant, for a day, and just to go through the assumptions in the business plan. It is much better to be caught short at this stage, rather than to find that later, you have a wrong assumption which affects major parts of the business plan. In the early stages of a business plan, 'guesstimates' as to the market size are acceptable. In many instances, in a developing market, an estimate will be all that there is to go on. However, it is important to identify key 'market drivers' and to monitor them closely, and to update the business plan regularly. As time goes on, an initial market size is gradually turned into a sales forecast.

This comment about industry consultants, is important for the smaller companies, who maybe do not have the breadth of industry experience, in a new market. To employ an expert, for a day, who can question the assumptions and provide a wealth of industry knowledge and contacts is money well spent. Many government-led initiatives allow the smaller company to employ consultants for just this sort of work and their advice can be invaluable. They can also become part of the devil's advocate department.

Exposing potential customers

Proactive telephone calling can often help to expose some potential customers. If the product is a new product in a new market sector, the use of co-partner companies whose knowledge of that sector is much better can be a real benefit. It is significant in the 1994 Queen's Awards for Technological Achievement, that of the 15 winners, 3 winners were partnerships between 2 companies in each case, complementing each others' technical, marketing and sales skills.

Quality market research

It cannot be emphasised enough. The better the quality of the market research, at this stage, the better understood is the whole opportunity, and hence the better the quality of the scheme. **Probably this is the single most important thing which the marketing department will do during the scheme. It can be the make or break of the potential product.**

MARKET RESEARCH OBJECTIVES

To help with shaping up the business opportunity, here are some ideas:

- Market history
- Past growth rates, future anticipated growth rates
- Competitor companies
- Competitive technologies
- Competitor product analysis – strengths and weaknesses
- Profit margins, sales channels and discount/incentive structures

- Peculiarities of market, technical and commercial
- Market drivers and third-party influences which affect market. Regulatory bodies etc.
- End user feedback

The results will influence the product(s) designs and hence the shape of the whole project.

Market research plan

The market research plan is therefore vital and it is important that a list of objectives is created so that the input is tailored to give answers to the objectives. Technical and production involvement is key as they will want questions answered which will not be obvious to the marketing department. It does not matter whether the product is a physical item or a piece of paper like a pension plan or life assurance policy, researching the market, and looking at what the opposition is up to is a vital means of providing input to allow the design of a product which should be as good or better than the opposition. The opposition may be similar products, or may be competing technologies. In the final event the decision to buy or not to buy will be taken by the consumer, or end user. The more understanding as to why a competitor's product is bought, the better the design of your own product.

Pre-launch plan

The writing of a pre-launch plan may seem very premature. However, it is a good exercise as it indicates what needs to be done by whom, when and why. For example you may have decided that the product is needed to replace an existing product, which is losing market share to the competition. You need to set a provisional launch date, and then set milestone events back from that date to where you are now. This gives everyone a clear idea of what needs to be done.

Research and development

Research and development may be experimenting with a number of different variances, and they need to be given clear guidance to look at health and safety issues, as this may preclude certain options at an early stage and prevent later and costly revision work when a component is found to be unacceptable. If there are several product variances, they may need again to be exposed to some basic user trial, or exposed to their production colleagues, as some variants may be far less costly to make, than others.

Production

Production should be able to give a clear indication of its supply lines unless the product is new to the company and thus may require new suppliers, who need to be identified, qualified, and brought on board.

Bear in mind that engineering estimates with regard to timescales are often very optimistic, and it is worth doubling the estimates on timescales, unless the estimate is very clearly right, or the supplier is well-known to perform within these deadlines. When this work has been done, then there is an opportunity review, which looks at the scale of the opportunity, and firms up the initial figures. If the decision is taken to go on, the action plan needs to be agreed at the review as it will have to be funded with resources, and as the product goes on, more people will be involved. The action plan for Stage 2 is probably the most critical, as this stage is essentially make or break.

Checks and balances

In any company there will be a set of checks and balances, which allows money, time, and people to be set to work on various projects. Any new product or service is created by an individual or a team, and then is sold to those who have the power to allocate resources. To a certain extent a buyer–seller relationship exists, even though in many cases the two are on the same side within the company. In other situations, the buyer may actually be a merchant bank, a venture capital organisation or a local high street bank manager. In any event, there is a series of fundamental points which exist from both the buyer and seller points of view. It is very helpful if each side understands the other's perspective. These can be summarised as follows:

SELLERS:

Typically the product team

- **Does this fit the present business strategy?**
  - Does it fit into existing product/market group?

- Is it innovative and why?
- Does it meet customer/and or market needs?
- Does it replace/enhance or kill existing product?
- Is the product sustainable?

- **Have we got the right skills to make the product a success?**
  - Have our past efforts resulted in growth?
  - Do we have a climate within the company that supports innovative ideas? If not how do we encourage that climate?
  - Have we got the systems and procedures to make the product a success?

- **Are we sufficiently innovative?**
  - Have we got both evolutionary and revolutionary ideas on the product?
  - Are there funds available and are they apportioned to new and existing products?

- **Have we got a balance between low-risk, medium-risk and high-risk products?**
  - Can we identify the risks, rewards and timings?
  - Any conflict with other projects?

- **What financial impact will the project have?**
  - What return will we get over what timescale?
  - Do we have sufficient cash flow to fund the project.
  - If not how do we proceed?

- **Can we achieve our goals with an external partner company?**
  - Do we need help with markets/technical/funds/other?

BUYERS:

Board of Directors, New Products Committee, or external funds source

- **Is the company using innovation to enhance its business strategy and competitive edge?**
  - How innovative are we; what is its role within the company?
  - How does the project fit within the company's strategy?
  - Is there a good fit with markets, other products, capital and investment plans?

- **Do the risks/rewards give a long-term revenue value?**
  - What will be the impact on earnings, cash flow and capital?
  - How valuable are the potential opportunities?
  - What is the real risk?
  - If we miss the opportunity how serious will it be to our future?

- **How realistically have the risks been assessed?**
  - Do we use SWOT* analysis?
  - Have we a previous record of high-risk development?
  - Are the risks customer, market or technically related?

- **Are the potential plans for the project viable?**
  - Is the project/management team capable?
  - Is the team balanced?
  - Is the idea/product balanced?
  - Has the company got the necessary human skills/resources to deliver the product?
  - If not, can it get them?
  - What's the company track record on new products? Can it be improved?
  - What capital is needed?
  - Any spin-off to other products?

* **SWOT** analysis stands for Strengths, Weaknesses, Opportunities and Threats

SAMPLE ACTION LIST

Note that actions are clearly agreed with the person concerned and a reporting timescale set up.

1 TR to draw up brief market research survey for meeting 5.11.94
   (a) TR to contact sales dept at next sales meeting on 24.10.94
   (b) BB to contact Action Distribution Ltd with regard to their knowledge of EC markets
   (c) TR to contact Alan Try Consultants for one-day initial market survey
   (d) Tracy to visit County Hall archives for European statistics
   (e) Tracy to obtain from US Embassy library the US market statistics
   (f) Agreed world demand is approx. (EC+US) x 1.5
   (g) BB to segment market into industrial and retail with distribution channels (see RG) 28.11.94

2 DRC to produce samples by hand for 'show and tell'. Ideally one for sales meeting on 24.10. Report 5.11.94

3 DRC to estimate costs based on semi-automated production with volume 0.5 per cent of world demand 5.11.94

4 DRC to estimate cost based on automated production based on 2 per cent of estimated world demand 5.11.94

5 DRC to provide capital costs on plant in both cases, with time-scales to completion, and benefits to other products with plant expansion 28.11.94

6 BB to produce sales price list based on competition and work back to make price. Work with AD to compare trade and retail margins 5.11.94

7 DRC to arrange brief technical assessment of Proton and Gains Inc. units with advantages and disadvantages 28.11.94

8 BB to obtain 7 end users who will be prepared to try the handmade samples and comment. Report 5.11.94

9 TR to write outline business plan with Lan Hardman in accounts. Lotus 123 standards apply 5.11.94

10 TR to get 'guesstimate' of packaging costs for home and export, both as packed by competitors, and in proposed new cardboard format. TD in production to estimate labour costs in both types 28.11.94

It is good practice to circulate the action list not only to the team members, and co-opted team members, but also to their line managers and senior management. It is of great help in ensuring that members are not expected to do more than two days' work in a single day!

MARKET RESEARCH OBJECTIVES CHECKLIST

- Market history

- Past growth rates, future anticipated growth rates

- Competitor companies

- Competitive technologies

- Competitor product analysis – strengths and weaknesses

- Profit margins, sales channels and discount/incentive structures

- Peculiarities of market, technical and commercial

- Market drivers and third-party influences which affect market. Regulatory bodies etc.

- End user feedback

- Whether the market sector(s) are expanding, static, or contracting

- Statutory regulations. Overseas regulations. Overseas test requirements. Health and safety standards.

The results will influence the product(s) designs, and hence the shape of the whole project.

Statistics

During a project the author was asked to help in assembling market information on a new technical product to be sold in the consumer market. We looked at a range of consumer electronic products all of which showed exactly the same uptake rates. Sales of black and white TV sets in the 1950s in the US had exactly the same uptake curves as colour TVs, video cameras, microwave ovens, personal computers, dishwashers etc.

What was also interesting was that many industrial products follow the exact same pattern. So therefore in the prediction of a potential new market, it may be possible to consider an existing product, or another product in the same market and predict the same growth curve. For example, the office microcomputer was strictly an office product for the first ten years of its life. Its mathematics of uptake was exactly the same as the domestic video recorder or dishwasher.

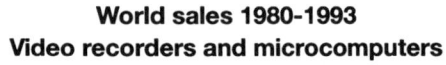

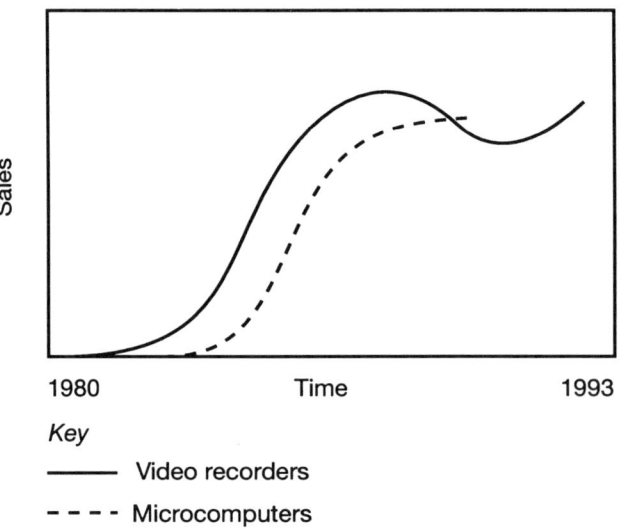

World sales 1980-1993
Video recorders and microcomputers

Key
———— Video recorders
- - - - Microcomputers
NB: Blip in video recorder due to sale of second unit

Outline design

Research and development may be experimenting with a number of different variances, and they need to be given clear guidance to look at health and safety issues, as this may preclude certain options at an early stage and prevent later and costly revision work, when a component is found to be unacceptable. If there are several product variances they may need again to be exposed to some basic user trial or exposed to their production colleagues as some variants may be far less costly to make than others. The outline design will need to be dovetailed with the product proposal plan. To a certain extent this plan is a wish list. What may be desirable may not be economic, feasible, or produceable. As this is a very early stage there is no need to fix a specification, so flexibility is the key.

Patents, trademarks and copyrights

Patent and trademark issues should be looked at, if relevant, as should the myriad of government, EC and other trade regulations. If exporting the product to other markets it is essential that all relevant regulations are understood at an early stage, and the 'tightest' of the specifications selected to test against. If, for example California is proposing some new health regulations which are not law now but could be shortly, then it is wise to regard them as *fait accompli* as they are likely to be adopted ultimately in the US, and then as a *de facto* standard in other countries. Adopting test standards early helps reduce costs later on, and prevents the embarrassing silence when a product is found either not conforming to a country's specification or has not been tested.

Supply lines and partnerships

Production should be able to give a clear indication of its supply lines unless the product is new to the company, and thus may require new suppliers, who need to be identified, qualified, and brought on board.

Bear in mind that engineering estimates with regard to timescales are often very optimistic, and it is worth doubling the estimates on timescales, unless the estimate is very clearly right, or the supplier is well known to perform within these deadlines.

Gate review

When this work has been done, then there is an opportunity review, which looks at the scale of the opportunity, and firms up the initial figures. At the end of Stage 1, the gate review will need to have a detailed action list with costings, timing and resources needed, if it passes to Stage 2. If the decision is taken to go on the action plan needs to be agreed at the review as it will have to be funded with resources, and as the product goes on, more people will be involved. The action plan for Stage 2 must be prepared in advance, so that time loadings are understood for the team participants, and budgets and timescales agreed with department heads.

SITUATION 6

You are sitting on the NPC. R&D budgets are tight, as the company is weathering the recession and the profits are dramatically down. You receive two different product proposals from the NPS.

Product 1

In the industrial division your company has been making industrial racking for many years. Changes in both types of products and safety considerations have led the group to suggest the use of preformed plastics. These result in a corrosion-resistant shelf, which is considerably lighter, but with the same loadbearing capability as steel. The team has presented a basic outline of its idea and a small amount of seedcorn cash has gone into getting more information.

The team has given an idea of the market size, and savings in material and production costs and has identified better margins for the product. The company has no history of plastic processing, and so will need to make major capital investments in plant and tooling. The risk is regarded to be medium to high, and the rewards are regarded as being medium to high.

The team has written an action plan which calls for a more detailed investigation of the plant and tooling needed and the production of some product to test in conjunction with a co-operative manufacturer of the plastic processing machinery.

Q? *Your decision is to Stop – Hold – Go On?*

Product 2

A subsidiary company that largely wholesales bought-in products from elsewhere has, for the last few years, been selling an American-made product. This product has sold well and is a simple 'hammer-in steel spike, which allows a wooden fence post to be bolted or fixed in'. This product has had moderate increase in sales but has suffered recently due to adverse £ to $ exchange rates.

Another group in the industrial division has also got seedcorn funding for the investigation. It reports that the product can easily be made using existing plant. Manufactured cost is below the current cost of buy-in price and sea shipping. Based on existing demand, it can utilise the existing workforce and take on five new workers to meet order requirements. Its action plan requires some money to build a few α test prototypes, and to establish optimum production techniques. BS5750 write-ups will be needed. If adopted, the industrial products plant will be fully loaded. The project is regarded as low risk, and the rewards are only moderate.

Q? *Your decision is to Stop – Hold – Go On?*

SITUATION 7

Your Role: You are from the marketing department of a video wholesaler.

You are making a Gate 1 proposal to the NPC.

History so far
You are the product champion. On a visit to the USA, you encountered several large video stores which had very upmarket sales areas, renting not only video products, but also selling CD ROMS, and computer software. These stores were strategically sited, enjoyed high shopper populations and were profitable.

Sanity check results
Your sanity checks reveal that there is a good potential business in the UK. It has not been done before. The marketplace is changing to multimedia. Home computer ownership is said to be higher per capita than the USA. Your company has sanctioned some funds to expand and firm up the business opportunity.

Next steps
You need to establish a number of basic facts:

1 That an expanded and upmarket store sells considerably more £s per sq. metre
2 That there is not another competitive high street retail channel for CD ROMs and computer software
3 That you are able to compete on price and performance with other sales channels
4 That you can buy/lease small-sized supermarkets which have been superceeded
5 That customers are prepared to drive to you rather than the local video store
6 That you can offer a wider range of video hire products as well as other software
7 You need to identify a computer software distributor who can provide their portfolio of products

Q? *What is now needed to prove the points above? What is the action plan to Gate 2?*

8

STAGE 2 – BEFORE GATE 2:
Defining and Justifying the Product

In the late 1970s the only way computer printouts could be printed was on expensive line printers (upper case only) teletype printers, fledgling dot matrix printers and daisywheel printers. All had their uses but had limitations in speed and fonts; they produced a lot of noise. A major computer company developed a system of using a resistive ribbon to deposit ink onto the page, which was much quieter than a dot matrix printer and gave output which was as good as a daisywheel printer with the capability of doing more than one font. It clearly was a new product which neatly dropped into the office marketplace on any computer system. The product was developed and launched in the early 1980s but sales were disappointing.

COMMENT

The reason was that at the same time, the laser printer had been developed. This competing technology was much faster, and more flexible than the resistive ribbon printer. It used single sheets of paper the same as the office photocopier, and could do good-quality graphics. Prices were similar between the competing technologies.

*The product failed the **Right Time** test. Launched earlier, it would have made inroads into the fledgling dot matrix and the daisywheel markets, but was unable to compete strongly with the laser printer.*

*It may also have failed **Right Price**. If priced between the laser printer and the dot matrix/daisywheel printer then it may have produced a much better market share.*

Stage 1 has firmed up the opportunity, but there still will be many questions that are unanswered and which need to be solved. The definition of the product will often help in solving these problems and also will allow the team and the company to assess the risk in terms of capital, time, and people employed versus the reward factor.

In all companies, resources are finite. Hence, if the company commits itself at this stage to a project, it will by necessity be precluding itself from several alternative projects that may be just as worthy. If the company backs a loser, then it loses not only that project, but also the chance of an alternative project, which has already been ousted by the loser, becoming a success.

Justification

Therefore, the justification part of this project is vital. The devil's advocate needs to be very active here, and needs to be teasing out of the participants, alternative scenarios, a 'what if this or that' happens. He should be instigating several different versions of the business plans based on his comments. While he is a valuable member of the team, his alternative approaches aid the thinking, and possibly the blinkered mentality of the product champion.

The business plan needs to be written up in some detail, and needs to look at important factors such as faster than anticipated growth, slower growth, faster price attrition by the competition, effect of delays on the project, etc. While this sounds a daunting task, with modern spreadsheets and microcomputers it means only a few hours work on changing the parameters within the spreadsheets. This yields important results that quickly indicate the critical factors to be watched and understood. For example, the reduction in a competitor's selling price may affect margins to such an extent that the proposed selling price is high, therefore affecting the proposed margin structure, and the profitability of the product. This may mean redesigning the product to reduce the cost. Equally the reduction in price by a competitor may signal a rapid growth in the marketplace, resulting in the market expanding 200–300 per cent, which may impose a completely different scenario on the product. The quality of market research done earlier should be a great help in understanding the maturity of the market and hence the factors affecting the pricing.

For example, most consumer products varying from the TV set to the cellular telephone follow the same mathematical growth curves. If price is plotted against sales, there is a critical point at which, when prices fall beyond a certain point, exponential growth rates are achieved.

In another example, the microcomputer market tends to have a very poor sales record in the months May to September, resulting in component suppliers reducing price to stimulate demand. This in turn results in lower prices from September onwards. Every year this happens, and every year product managers ignore the historical records, and reduce their prices to stimulate demand. There is little evidence to suggest that they achieve lasting increases in sales, or increases in market share. It is therefore important that price reductions that are gradual and long-term reductions, are not confused with reduction in stocking or panic selling. Understanding of the market is paramount.

Marketing actions

Marketing, based on customer-led comments, and inputs from technical departments, needs to define some basic product specifications. Based on these specifications, prototypes (where possible) should be developed and then given to live customers for their reactions. In some instances, this may be activity in the form of a focus group.

Focus groups

Focus groups are assembled by an independent chairman and often have no idea of what they will be shown or asked to discuss or comment on. A typical focus group may be asked to comment on the ease of opening of a new screw bottle top, comparing it with existing type. Followed by comments on a new type of photographic paper where a number of the same images is presented using different types of paper. Then they may be asked to look at two different insurance policies and comment on which style of writing and format they like. Focus group members can be of two types: general and specific. The general types are mixed groups of ordinary people, whose attitudes are not dissimilar from that of the 'man on the Clapham omnibus'. A specialist group may be of persons with specific group interests. For example, a car accessory maker, may want his product shown to general groups to understand the typical car users' reaction and to special groups from car clubs, whose enthusiasm for the product may be different.

They will be selected by the chairman, and may be specialist or general according to the nature of the products. The presentation of the photographic papers to a group from local camera clubs may get a different reaction from a group selected from the local community centre, who do not have special photographic interests. Focus groups will tell it as they see it and many marketeers have been crucified by these groups because they are unbiased and they will not see what is 'obvious' to the marketeer!

Results

In the case of the 'send-only telephone' (see Chapter 2) focus groups did not think it was of interest because of cost and lack of convenience. If their comments had been heeded, £0.5bn would have been saved!

In Japan a series of focus groups looked at how the average owner understood the programming of video cassette recorders. Less than 8 per cent understood them and most regarded the system as far too complex. One member facetiously suggested that you should be able to shout at the thing to programme it! That idea was tried and proved to be very success-ful for the maker – but only in Japanese.

However, in many companies such activity is meaningless. Industrial companies, who have only a limited number of customers, know them well and are known by their customers, so that such focus group needs are not necessary.

Health and safety statement

By this time a health and safety statement needs to be made so that any issues are exposed and debated. In many such issues there will be a grey area. For example, the Ames test is much abused as a test, according to its inventor Professor Ames. Some countries will not allow any item which is Ames positive to be sold there, 'because it is carcinogenic'. This is a serious oversimplification, as the Ames test does not indicate direct car-cinogenicity and some carcinogens pass the Ames test while other items, such as foodstuffs and whisky, fail.

Equally, there will be qualification of the test results. For example, a rubber component in the carburettor of a car may fail the Ames test, but neither the carburettor nor the car will be seen as a threat because the rubber component would not come into near enough proximity to the driver to be any threat. Positive Ames tests invariably involve more detailed testing which takes time and money and at the end may still not give a definitive result. Where possible, select alternative materials, which do not have any doubts about their safety. If the doubtful material shows better technical performance it may well be a good idea to write parallel business plans. These take account of both scenarios, including delays due to the doubts on the 'better performer'.

In the vast majority of cases this process is a simple matter of common sense. However, all sorts of companies fall foul of such regulations, mainly because of a lack of thought. One such example was a typewriter company that thoughtfully provided a free sample of type correction fluid with the product. Some countries' customs officers refused entry to the product because the free sample did not have a 'solvent abuse sticker' on the bottle label. While this is trivial and nit-picking, the economic consequences of having a product stopped at customs is a major blow, and involves a lot of expensive remedial action. Rowntree Mackintosh, before they were taken over by Nestlé, suffered major problems with Smarties which had been marketed for many years in Europe, when they started sales in the US. The red button contained a dye which was FDA banned, though quite legal in Europe. They ended up selling Smarties without the red-coloured buttons! Such potential showstoppers are very expensive, and show that a lack of detailed preparation had taken place for the new market. Probably the best way forward for most companies, especially the smaller ones, is a trial sale. This tests everything associated with the product and means that all the regulations with regard to the country of import have been checked at the 'customs gate' before a full selling operation is underway.

Competitor analysis

Marketing needs to provide a competitor analysis and this is very important as the march of technology may provide a radically different way of doing the same thing. There are many cases of rival companies producing similar products, and some will have better performance yet lose out to their less well-performing rivals. One of the best examples was the video format Betamax, invented by Sony. Technically it was superior, but ultimately lost out to the inferior VHS system on commercial grounds. Some of the marketing input must take account of this and come to some conclusion as to the effect of the rival companies' image, branding etc. As competitor analysis is a continuing theme throughout the Scheme, it should be researched and revisited at every gate review. Competitor analysis clearly identifies competitors and their products. At each gate review, the new entrants to the market are an important pointer to its health and new products from competitors could steal the new product's thunder. Hence, it is important to have a quick review of competitors and their activities. If new and unusual activity is reported – investigate!

In the case of the printer maker mentioned in earlier chapters, his development of a new quiet printer was completely overshadowed by the development of the Xerographic laser printer. Such development should have been mooted as a major threat, because on a cost basis it was similar but had far superior performance. That company, was one of the last companies to embrace that technology, which was very surprising, considering its leading position in the computer market. Clearly there was a climate in the company that did not attach importance to the competitor technology. There should have been a quick focus group test because clearly the end user base was prepared to buy the competitor technology in far greater numbers. This should have sounded warning bells – it did not.

Competitor response

Part of that competitor analysis must look at the possible reactions of competitors to the product, which could include drastic price cuts and their possible new products. No one in the 1970s took the threat of Japanese car makers seriously. It was a mistake. Some major companies may be prepared to take a long-term view and will quite happily enter into a trade war, by slashing margins, to kill off a new competitor. In that instance it is vitally important that you know the exact cost of the new product and possibly have a 'cost reduction' team looking at ways of reducing costs even before launch has taken place. The company should have taken a view by the launch date how they would fight off a trade war, and preferably have some plan in outline at least.

Marketing plans

Having mapped out the pre-launch plan marketing will need a development stage plan, and possibly a follow-on product plan as well if this is relevant and possible. It should also be overseeing a cost reduction plan if relevant. It will also need to understand and implement any technical service needs, if relevant. If the product is being subjected to α and β testing, then the technical service department will be instrumental in controlling this. It should understand and analyse the results and feed them back to the R&D team. There is a lot of merit in having technical service for at least the α test. First, the product will be a prototype (and this may be a pension plan or insurance policy), and so the persons using the product will be unfamiliar with it, as will those in the 'selling structure'. Only a few R&D members will be *au fait*. Having a trained technical person to help the customers pays benefits in other ways. He will get direct customer feedback, suggestions for improvements, comments on competitors' products, which would not be forthcoming to the same extent. His input at the end of the α test, may well reshape the design of the product, in light of customer experience.

Product development

R&D will have developed the product to such a stage as to make the product demonstrable, and also produce such prototypes as can be used with customer interactions. This may sound easy – it usually is not.

R&D will have provided major input to marketing on the stages of the development plan, so that they should have their own agenda on development. R&D will also have responsibility to understand the legal position with regard to patents and trademarks. The R& D department of a finance house must understand the constantly changing legislation with regard to their new product whereas patents and trademarks would be irrelevant.

Production and engineering, will have had to look at manpower; plant needs versus plant capacity for the business plan. They will also have a much clearer idea on sourcing external components and packaging. They will need to provide an easily understood summary on the plant, and the demands that the new product could make. Also, they should look at external remedies on a short- or medium-term basis if relevant and be able to provide costings if the external route is indicated as a possibility. The production department should also be able to estimate the effect that the new product would have on other products being produced at the same time. This may be quite important, as if the product is disruptive, then this may dictate how and when it is produced, even to the extent of allowing another product to 'jump the queue' to launch, simply because it is less disruptive.

Finance should provide a preliminary financial plan, with profit and loss accounts, capital account and some first passes at cash flow forecasting. They must be intimately involved in the business plan and ideally should start to 'own' it. At the end of this stage, the project will pass to the development stage, where the product will receive substantial funding. **Beware, this stage is the most critical**. Flaws here will show up sooner or later!

SITUATION 8

Goldwell Chemical Company has made strides with its new product. It has identified a number of separate marketplaces, and forged good technical and commercial relationships with several major players in the markets. It has found that a number of technical problems have led to a change in the initial design. It has been found that iridium/zinc electrodes suffer from ageing, resulting in lower efficiency. An iridium/aluminium electrode works better and has greater longevity, but it delivers about 10 per cent less voltage.

Competitor analysis has revealed that silicon solar panels are inefficient. This is because the cells are circular which means a 17 per cent waste of linear surface area, which is not the case in the Goldwell cell, which is square. The lowered voltage in the Goldwell cell is balanced by its more efficient use of the available area for light collection and its conversion to electricity. Overall it is now believed that the Goldwell cell can be sold for about 12 per cent of the equivalent cost of the silicon competitor, on a voltage/sq. metre basis.

Dr Gaunt is asking for the product to be passed to Stage 2 so that it can be better defined and justified.

Q1 *What questions will you ask over performance of the Goldwell cell?*

Q2 *There appear to be a number of important features not mentioned in his proposal. What are they, and what do you want to see to allow things to proceed?*

Q3 *Gaunt has not defined his options with regard to going it alone, establishing licensees, or a combination of both . What would you do?*

Q4 *Assuming you pass the product to the next stage, what would the action plan look like?*

Q5 *What shape should the business plan be in by now?*

9

STAGE 3 – BEFORE GATE 3:
Developing the Product

CAUTIONARY TALE 9

The Channel Tunnel is rarely out of the news. On the start of regular passenger services it has been found that up to 10 per cent of the cars, vans and four-wheel-drive vehicles will not fit the wagons which were designed to transport them. Problems of two types exist. First, some vehicles are 'too low' and ground their exhausts and petrol tanks when loading. Second, four-wheel-drives and some vans, when fitted with roof racks, will not fit.

COMMENT

*The wagons do not meet **Right Product** criteria. Ferry companies have been handling exactly the same vehicle populations and that includes air ferries. Clearly a lack of testing and understanding of the market resulted in poor design specifications. Clearly no proper α or β testing had taken place.*

The most popular selling car the Ford Mondeo, when fully laden with wine from a French supermarket, 'grounds' when loading. In any design criterion, it is not unreasonable to expect the most popular selling car to be fully laden when going on holiday, or returning from it.

GENERAL

The development stage is where considerably more resources are needed and where time and money will be important. At this stage almost all the functions will be expanding their needs. Marketing will be doing more field-based work. Technical will be building product for α testing, and production will be starting to produce trial product. The warehouse and packaging departments will start to get involved. Development is the stage where prototypes or precursors are made into a form where they are able to demonstrate all the features and benefits of the product or service.

At each stage there needs to a number of important feedback loops. These are not in the system to slow down the project. They should help to increase the speed of the process. As the production of the product takes place it becomes increasingly important that the R of R&D, is very much reduced, and the development is frozen so that the product can be productionised. However, the key to this is the α test. It is important to freeze the development of the product at a stage, because, human nature being what it is, there will be a continual process of adding improvements. These may delay the productionisation of the process or add extra production cost with any discernible user benefit. For example, the very complicated microwave ovens sold very well in the early stages of the market, but market research shows that experienced users, when buying new microwaves, choose a much more basic model. This means that either they do not value some of the sophisticated options or they do not know how to use them!

The α test takes the product that you think you want to make (and think you can make), builds a limited number, and then lets a small select group of customers use the product. This will usually require some technical hand holding if the product is at all technical. However, the object is to understand what problems the prototype may cause the customer and then to fix them. It is essential at this stage that as much time and money is taken as necessary to ensure that this test is done properly, and to ensure that a representative sample of customers is also representative of the uses and ranges of conditions the product will work in. If a chocolate maker produces a new snack product, it is essential that it is tested for durability and taste in both the temperate and tropical markets. It may well require two formulations, for higher and lower temperatures, in order to avoid a 'concrete' product which breaks false teeth in winter, and a 'semi liquid' product which leaks everywhere in summer.

To return to the bank account example, if, for example, the customer is given his new account and finds that he cannot pay standing orders, it should have been fixed at the α test stage.

Competitive activity

Hand in hand with such development work will need to be a better understanding of the responses and the changes to the marketplace. Technology seems to run relentlessly on, so that many market opportunities that were large at the start of the scheme may have significantly changed by the time Gate 3 is encountered. This may be due to similar companies having the same idea, or similar, and there may be emerging technologies which provide the solution in a different way.

The importance of market feedback

The marketing department and its sales 'eyes and ears' need to monitor shows, conferences, trade press and the gossip from its sales and distribution arms to constantly understand and monitor threats to the product. If a serious threat is mounted it may be cheaper to discontinue the project and go onto the next. On the other hand, the threat must be fully evaluated technically and commercially before action is taken. In the short term this may be impossible and so some real decisions may have to wait for better information.

Business plan

The business plan should now be full blown, and have inputs from all sources with as few guesstimates as possible. Regular 'what if' scenarios should be run to see if changes in market size, pricing, etc. will benefit the business and what effect slower and faster take up will have on the business It will also be very helpful if the market size is monitored, because if it is expanding or contracting fast, this will have a major effect.

Customer feedback

Customer feedback must be widely circulated (good and bad news). There is a lot of benefit at this stage of informal 'crystal ball gazing', between all departments, and all their employees. With larger companies such activities are a good boost to morale and also it is surprising how many good ideas come from humble foot soldiers, which benefits the project.

After weeks of thought an industrial packaging problem was debated without any good solution. This was mentioned at a brainstorming session and the result was an outstanding industrial packaging solution. It came from a process worker who had had an Indian take-away the night before, and understanding the problem, the application of a 'take-away'-like container solved both commercial and technical problems at a stroke. This blinding flash of inspiration was to the embarrassment of the packaging specialist (the author) whose response was 'why did we not think of that?'

The α test

The alpha test is a critical stage of the new product and it is vital that it is done right. Done wrongly, the product may appear to be too difficult to make at the right price, or may be assumed to be easy to make, but found to have too many shortcomings. The alpha test product should, as far as possible, be more or less what is expected to be marketed. For example, if an electronic product, it can be 'breadboard' handmade boards, and the enclosures can be handmade.

If an insurance policy it needs to be handled in a different way.

The alpha test rules need to be laid down as follows:

- Must be as close as possible to the proposed end result (can be handmade)
- Must be fully operational so that customers can use all the features
- Must not have features which will be in the β test product, but are absent here (unless the test indicates need for improvements)
- Must be introduced by sales/technical departments, and installed and training provided for customers where relevant, as there are unlikely to be installation and user manuals
- Must be subject to regular user feedback by personal or telephone contact
- Must be supported by telephone or field technical support if needed
- May need to be redesigned, upgraded or modified in light of customer critique
- Must be exposed to critical comment in light of competitors' products, new products, new applications
- Must be subject to market testing in different markets, and must be seen as a different 'product', if different markets give a very different level of response

- If relevant should be shown to customer focus groups for their reactions.

At the end of the alpha test, there will be some serious pointers which will come out and they should be checked as follows:

- Success of design or more work needed
- Response of different markets – will the same product work? Product variances
- Customer response good or would be good if faults rectified
- Product can be made closely to alpha test prototypes by the production team at the proposed costs
- Sample product delivers the expectations and features claimed and is liked by sample customers, representing real benefits or advances on what they use at the moment.

Another alpha test may be needed if there is a serious product redesign and this will need to be retested in the market and exposed to the production team who will have to make it. In some very technical products several tests may be needed before the unit is passed as being the 'final design'. In some instances, it may be found that a different way of producing the product introduces changed features, which would need to be used by customers. If the new production technique introduces cost savings, this must be tested, and balanced against customer comment.

CASE STUDY

A vacuum cleaner maker produced a very successful upright cleaner for a number of years. In order to use the hose attachments a sub-assembly needed to be fitted to the base. This was seen as being ungainly, and a new product was designed and produced which was the same unit with the hose assembly built in. A simple lever moved the system from upright to hose operation. However, the system had 30 per cent less suction in 'upright mode', and the very small airways provided for the hose operation frequently became blocked. The product did not do well.

More careful α testing of the product, and allowing customers to test and use both the older and newer product, would have showed up the design faults before the product was mass produced.

Genuine customer reaction

Both the gatekeeper and the devil's advocate need to ensure that customer reaction is as reported and that genuine problems and criticisms are given the same weight as favourable comment. This is the right time to critically examine the product and the input of customer comment is essential, as correction of design problems later will be very costly. In some α testing, it is often worth using an internal panel of non-specialists to look at a product and to make critical comment. The secretary, tea person or fork-lift truck driver will tend to have an earthy opinion on the product and point out weaknesses that may be overlooked by people who are closer to the product. Sometimes it is also worth telling them that it is from a third party, as they will tend to be more truthful in their critique.

SUCCESS STORY

A car maker was crucified by an internal review committee of non-specialists, for putting the electric window up/down buttons so far back on the central console that the driver could not see them when driving the car. They moved them to the door position where this manufacturer always now positions them. Their competitors still place these switches in a variety of different and inaccessible positions.

Negative comments

Done properly, the α test should output a successful design that will go to production, be made successfully and become a profitable product for the company. At this stage negative consumer comments should not stop the project but rather work should be done to eliminate the problems that caused the comments.

In the case of the small photocopier manufacturer, the α test results were dire. The product, as it then existed, was unsaleable. The subsequent fix of the problem is classic. Apart from fixing a major technical problem, it also introduced a major long-term revenue stream from the sales of consumable toner cartridges which did not exist before. This must have made a major impact on the company bottom line and its distributors.

While at the prototype stage it is worth looking again at any regulations that the product is likely to have to meet, specially with regard to health and safety, electrical, VDE, IMRO, LAUTRO and other regulatory bodies. If the product is to be exported to different countries, the need is to make to the tightest world specification, rather than the local one, because failure of a tighter specification will mean redesign or preclusion from that market. It may be required even in the local market at a later stage. It should also be checked that production products meet the same specifications as handmade pre-production prototypes.

α test support

Unlike the β test, it is quite permissible for the prototypes to be released into the field, with the product needing technical support. At this stage this may be critical and will provide an important feedback in understanding how the customers both use and abuse the product. One computer keyboard maker was quite surprised to find that many of his keyboards stopped working when coffee is spilt into them!

The technical staff in such a job should be trained to be diplomatic and not discuss the project because some comments will be reported to the competition. However, as much field contact as possible should be encouraged at this stage, as variance in the product's use needs to be understood. If variance is important, some statistical sampling should be done to identify the β test sites later on. The right personalities selected for technical service can build good personal relationships with their customers, that can provide invaluable feedback. Some important information on competitors' products performance relative to the α test sample can be obtained. While marketing can do some of the competitor information and the R&D department can evaluate competitor products, the input from customers' sites where the two products are in use side by side is invaluable. It can, in some cases, result in the repositioning of the product in the market.

Other activities

In the R&D department a full product specification should exist, and this should be passed to the production department, again with the clear understanding that the specifications may change in light of α test input. The R&D department should be providing a complete technical analysis of the relevant competitors' products. Marketing should be able to add numbers to them, including end user pricing, estimated margins, volumes and any reported field problems. Smaller companies obviously cannot afford much time in assessing competitors' products, but often a technical person can be shown a competitor's product and very quickly come up with an assessment that is surprisingly accurate. Any such feedback is better than none. In such situations, the classic 'compare and contrast' technique should be used, producing at least five 'points of difference'.

Production should be starting to 'own' the specification and should have completed a complete production assessment and have clear ideas of which processes are going to be the limiting factors to the overall output. How they will overcome any such bottlenecks needs to be addressed. They should be looking at alternate scenarios, including short and medium term, outplacing of work, cost variances, plant costs, plant loadings, etc.

Finance should be intimately involved in the project and should be revising the Stage 2 finance plan, and be providing important input into the business plan.

SITUATION 9

Andrews & Porlock Ltd, a long-term maker of small domestic appliances is proposing to launch a new vacuum cleaner. Stages 1 and 2 have been passed successfully, and Dave Gray, the R&D Manager is very pleased that his idea of a microporous disposable vacuum bag has worked well. R&D tests show that this is collecting pollen and similar-sized grains, which most vacuum cleaners are unable to collect. Initial feedback from customers in the α test, reveals that they like the product, and are prepared to pay a premium for its superior 'lust for dust'.

Kevin Smith, a technical service engineer, has reported strong interest from a distributor, who sells products into industrial areas, following an α test at one of the distributors' customer sites. Kevin says 'We apparently have a completely new market. The medical market needs a system that can vacuum up items like dust mites which are a major cause of allergies and a major problem for hospitals and nursing homes. In addition the distributor reports strong demand for such a product from companies in the industrial area that work in 'clean room' conditions and these include medical products makers, pharmaceutical companies, electronics companies and instrument makers. I see this market acting as a draw through for the general consumer market, because allergy sufferers will buy our products if they know these are available'.

Q1   *Has the company got its market right? Should it reposition on the market Kevin reports?*

Q2   *If they do reposition, comment on the technical and marketing changes needed.*

Q3   *What further actions would you insist on before going to Stage 4?*

10

STAGE 4 – BEFORE GATE 4:
Pre-launch

CAUTIONARY TALE 10

A relatively small toy maker in the US produced a new toy which was the 'hit' of the Consumer and Electronic Show in Chicago in 1992. Spectacular advance orders were received resulting in the company having to ramp up production and hire another 85 workers to meet demand. As the product was to be exposed to children in the age groups of 4–14 years, the Food and Drug Administration in the US vetoed the type of plastic used in the housing, as it was not safe if sucked by a smaller child, potentially imparting barium filler to the child.

COMMENT

*The company was unfortunate. It had failed to check that the plastics used in production were FDA approved. The product therefore failed **Right Production**. Luckily it was able to reformulate its plastics quite quickly but still suffered a four-month delay on launch while the FDA gave approval to the product in its modified form.*

GENERAL

The passage to Stage 4 means that the product is on track to be launched, subject to certain 'showstoppers' that will be obvious. At this stage the company will have all departments working hard to ensure that the product will succeed. Research and development will by now be winding down their major activities, while production, packaging, warehousing and the sales teams will be working hard to ensure that it succeeds. Finance and marketing will be working to finish a robust business plan, with forward sales forecasting, so that their production colleagues know potentially what volumes to make and on what timescales. The pre-launch phase needs to include putting in place the 'evangelisation' of the product. Sir Clive Sinclair for example always seems to get very good advance publicity (at no cost to him) for his various projects, from computers to electric bicycles. Such publicity has a very high impact on the general public, is memorable, and needs careful planning to be a success. While most products are unlikely to end up on the front pages of national newspapers there is no reason why the planning of a press campaign cannot be enhanced by local radio/television publicity. Many early evening local news magazine-type programmes, are often looking for a 2-3 minute 'filler' about a local company. New products of almost any type are newsworthy. The same applies to trade magazines, which normally are very happy to publicise new products in their new product features. If going down this route it is well worth speaking to the editor personally, rather than just sending in a press release. The editor will be able to tell you exactly what he is looking for and may actually want to do a more detailed feature than simply a brief new product news release. In some trade and consumer products, user reviews can be of major benefit to the product. Such reviews do not cost the company much in terms of money, but can make a remarkable difference to the product launch. A beneficial review can have a major effect on trade channels and their order volumes. Small companies with innovative products can find that the 'Editor's Choice' accolade can transform their market positioning.

Showstoppers

For example, there may be a launch of a competitive technology that may make the product uncompetitive, or a change in the marketplace. The product may not be able to deliver a key feature and so may have to be delayed, but in general the company should be working toward a full launch of the product. A change in statutory regulations may change the product or part of it. The decisions at this stage are clear. The options are either 'cancel the complete programme'(which is going to be costly) or put the project on hold pending clarification, partial redesign, or continue.

This is a very difficult position in the product's progress. To stop the programme loses the company a lot of time and money and possibly leaves a hole in its product range, so allowing a competitor to jump into the space. On the other hand, to spend further money on a product which may never fulfil its potential may actually be more costly.

We have already considered the cases of the printer overtaken by new technology, the video camera launched into the wrong marketplace, both of which 'faults' would have surfaced at this stage in the product development cycle. Both products were technically good yet the printer never fulfilled its true potential. The video still camera is an emerging product, hence the decision to reposition the product was undoubtedly correct, as the market was new and will emerge as technology advances. In the case of the 'call-only cellular phone' stopping at this stage would have saved the four companies concerned about £500m. Had they believed their own market research, the projects should have been cancelled earlier, saving even more money.

At this point there needs to be a lot of soul-searching within the core team. Its members will have put in a lot of time and effort and should be given every opportunity to turn round the problem. At this stage the 'judge and jury' should also be intimately involved, as it is important that the decision is right. Showstoppers can be classified into different areas:

- Regulations, patents, trademarks, copyrights and health and safety problems
- Superior competitive technology
- Production problems
- Customer problems.

Regulations

The failure of a product to meet a local specification health regulation can be very serious. Time and money could however allow the regulations to be met or the product redesigned to comply.

Patent infringements are inevitable, as some companies may genuinely have developed a novel idea, only to find that another company has had the same idea elsewhere. Most companies in this situation will be prepared to license their patents at comparatively small cost, if their licensee is not a direct competitor. Even in direct competition, some industries, such as chemical and pharmaceutical, will be prepared to license a competitor to gain overall market share. Informal approaches (without lawyers) can usually test the water, before a formal approach is made.

Superior technology

If a major competitor has suddenly surfaced and this is seen as a threat, it may be necessary to conduct consumer-based focus groups to compare the two technologies. The output from this, and direct comparisons of the technical performance of the competitor (by R&D), should allow the threat to be quantified.

There are a number of historical cases (such as Betamax v. VHS) where the technological superior has been ousted by superior marketing. In such a situation an assessment of key market drivers may provide the product with a competitive edge without the need for technological superiority.

Production problems

The production problem is either a permanent stop on the product or it can be overcome. It can be overcome either by redesigning the product to produce it in a different way or by investment in superior plant to overcome the difficulty.

Customer problems

The most difficult problem is the fact that customers will not buy the product. In the case of the 'call-only cell phone' the results are history. In many other new products, the product itself may be creating a new market. Such a response may not be abnormal at this stage. β testing and further focus group testing may be needed to convince all the parties that the product is worth continuation.

If customers will not buy, it is vital to find out why. (This will also suggest that earlier gate reviews have not properly identified customer features and benefits.) The crucial decision is then whether the product can be repositioned to satisfy the customer needs, or whether the product is better cancelled.

Market plans

Market plans will be advanced. Marketing and sales will have a clear idea of what, where and when they will place product and, importantly, in what volumes. Sales forecasting will be well under way. The product will be fully described in a specification sheet. In other words, the product design will have been frozen. This may sound obvious, but there is a very strong temptation to squeeze in extra features, and this is usually driven by R&D and marketing. Resist this! If customer reaction is 'I can get this feature and benefit from a rival product, and without which I would not consider buying the product', the product needs to be recycled, so that the implications of the customer reaction are assessed. This needs further market input: a very clear idea of how the product needs to be redesigned and how it will be produced. The obvious case here is the 'call-only mobile telephone'.

It is far more important that the new product is fully productionised, rather than be further delayed by marginal specification changes, which may not be reproducible on the plant, or deliverable in terms of financial regulations if a financial product. Tactics at this stage may suggest that a follow-on product may be needed to maintain the sales momentum. In software sales the resale of an upgrade product is a very good contributor to the bottom line, when the features are mainly minor bug fixes, and few notional 'new features'. Many companies would do well to emulate such clever marketing. Motor car manufacturers have been clever to produce a range of products which are hierarchical in nature and which in fact have only simple cosmetic changes, but which are perceived to offer more luxurious motoring. This gives a motorist an uplift in image, if he has got a 'GL' rather than an 'L', when the same vehicle gets him from A to B in exactly the same manner.

The marketing and R&D departments should have completed a comprehensive assessment of both the commercial and technical aspects of the competitors' products, and their ability to deliver them into the relevant supply channels. Do not overlook such aspects as price tariffs, import duty etc., because this can influence the pricing policy for the product.

Patents etc.

A good look at the patent position and any relevant copyright and trademarks issues is important to ensure that any changes since you last looked are not going to cause showstoppers.

CASE STUDY

Microsoft produced their version of DOS 6.0 using patented algorithms that were owned by another company. That version of the operating system had problems directly related to the algorithms, resulting in severe loss of users' data files. This version was replaced by DOS 6.2 (a bug fix update) which was a free issue and must have cost $ millions to bring to market. They were then sued by Stac Products, who owned intellectual property rights to the algorithms and, who gained the net sum of $94m for patent infringement and forced Microsoft to completely withdraw the product and replace it with DOS 6.21 which was the same system minus the offending algorithms. The costs again, of withdrawing the product and replacing it with yet another version, must have run in tens of millions of dollars. In all, it is estimated that Microsoft must have lost all the profits from its sales and probably from previous versions of the product in replacement costs, lost inventory, penalties, and loss of face. A clear hard look at the patent position should have flagged a 'showstopper' situation which would have saved several hundred million dollars. In any such situation, there is always a pressure to 'go on and be damned'. Such a decision should also be tempered with the knowledge of what such a decision may cost, and in this case a delay of a few months would not have had a major effect on its leading market position, nor would it have made a huge hole in its bank account. The wrong decision, cost the company major amounts in fiscal terms. It also resulted in a major loss of face from producing DOS 6.0, which was unreliable and the bug fix 6.2, which worked OK, only to be withdrawn because it infringed Stac patents. In the US it started the debate about Microsoft's predominance in the marketplace, and calls have been made to break the company up, because it is said to be 'anticompetitive'. While this may be an exceptional case, where there are legal, patent or copyright issues, the costs of litigation and compensation are very high.

CASE STUDY

Kodak was involved in a similar position with regard to its infringement of the patents held by Polaroid for the Land camera. Kodak spent $ millions in promoting its product, only to be defeated in the US courts with regard to patent infringement. The costs ran into $ billions for fees and penalties.

Production

The production department should have a contingency plan should a supplier fail for any reason whatsoever. It should prepare a clear list of what needs to be done, what improvements and changes are needed, and have clear plans for alternative sourcing of components. Production of a financial product will probably be limited to sales brochures, sales contracts etc. and similar plans should be prepared for service-based products. However, if they are not available at the right time, this clearly delays launch.

Engineering should have similar plans in order to deliver the appropriate changes in conjunction with the production department. Engineering should also be planning how to improve or cost reduce the product, so that as orderly production takes place, the economies of both scale and experience are put to good use, increasing margins by reducing manufacturing costs and failure rates.

Timing plan

Undoubtedly the company will have been using a timing plan from Gate 1 of the review. In the pre-launch stage the timing plan will be at its most critical. This is a very good means of ensuring that a whole range of activities take place simultaneously, and events that are critical are timed with sufficient leeway, to ensure that they do not cause a critical delay to other processes in the system. There is good software available to allow projects to be timed using a microcomputer.

CASE STUDY

In one project, the pre-launch plan involved a series of etched cylinders being made to support the printing of the product. A time of eight weeks was quoted by the UK-based supplier. Events proved that eight weeks was the timescale needed to do the job, but this was actually taking place in Germany. To get the product uplifted and transported to the UK took another ten days, and a further three days to get the cylinders mounted and the printing undertaken. In this instance it was wrong to assume an eight-week timescale; 10-11 weeks was more realistic.

It is important that timing plans take account of glitches, because at this stage of the project many of the suppliers are not well known to the company. It is prudent to include a measure of safety. Later on, once the companies have been doing business for some time, more accurate timescales may be built into the production plan.

Marketing and sales

Until now, the input of the sales department will have been limited to providing market intelligence, feeding information from the distribution network and providing customer sites.

Sales will now have to aim for a very strong presence with their own representative, rather than rely on the marketing department personnel, who generally have very limited selling experience. It is vital that from this stage onwards sales are *au fait* with the product and use all their expertise to sell it successfully.

Some very mediocre products, actually sell very well against better rivals, not due to their excellence, but rather due to the quality of the selling operation. The sales force are the commercial eyes and ears of the company and they will know better than anyone, both the customers and the competition. It is vital that they are allowed to control the selling operation and put in place the necessary initiatives to ensure the smooth running of the launch. This means, quite simply, that the process needs to start now.

Dependent on how the company does its selling will be the plan to ensure that the salespeople and their downstream sales processes are ready to go. This may involve dealers, distributors and therefore external sales teams. This may mean that the company's sales teams will have to learn how to train the external sales teams. If technical services are necessary this may mean the training of the internal technical services team, who in turn train the external ones. In any event any external salespeople will want sales literature, prices and point-of-sale material if needed.

Some products will need to be 'launched' at a show or exhibition. This means the planning of such a show, to ensure that the relevant sales channels are prepared. For example, a new investment package may need to be launched at a financial exhibition. This means that all the salespeople from third-party companies need to be invited to the stand and entertained. It may also be that the company wants to train them at a seminar, which can be incorporated into the schedule. If a product is launched at a show, this is an ideal opportunity to arrange good PR, so that visitors to the show can see the product for themselves. This is a very good opportunity to let both press and potential clients see the product working. It may, in some industrial situations, be the only chance. In many industrial markets, trade shows are often held every two or three years and advance planning is important, so that potential opportunities are not missed.

Regardless of shows, the PR system should be attempting to maximise the publicity potential of the launch in newspapers and periodicals. Bear in mind that most consumer research suggests that 'newspaper comment' on a product, is regarded as being three or four times more credible than the adverts, even if on the same page.

SUCCESS STORY

In one such instance, a small company launching a completely new car anti-theft device, used its distribution network salespeople. They targeted local newspaper stories over car thefts in their various areas and then arranged to write to the local papers, with a piece about the new product, and how it would have prevented the thefts. They wrote to 76 local papers around the country, and 75 per cent published stories on the new product completely free of charge!

Business plans

The business plan should be in daily use and be robust. Changes in the market state should be predicted on a 'what if' basis, and there should be alternative plans if conditions change seriously. The devil's advocate should be using the computer system to its full advantage, by predicting dire production problems due to failure of a supplier, for example, or temporary loss of markets due to war/strikes etc. Such exercises tease out of the company the critical factors that affect the product and allow some thought as to how these problems can be overcome. The 1973 oil crisis resulted in chaos round the world, not only because of the price of oil, but also due to its non-availability and that of the downstream chemical products. The situation affected all sectors of all economies. Many industries had to undergo reformulation, which meant major headaches for their downstream customers, because performance characteristics changed. Crises on the scale of the oil crisis are rare. Specific industry crises are less rare but often result in supply difficulties for months.

CASE STUDY

Two years ago a manufacturing plant in Japan that produces epoxy resins, practically blew up. It supplied 60 per cent of the world's resins used in the manufacture of computer memory. Prices tripled in 48 hours, and still have not returned to the previous levels. Suppliers who had alternative supply agreements, or were using a competitive supplier, were able to more than double their market share.

The innovative company will have planned and tested possible alternative components, if they are deemed to be at all critical. When such crises do occur, the innovative companies perform, and take a bigger market share, often maintaining it after the crisis has long gone.

Much very good work has been written on business plans, and most companies use the now ubiquitous spreadsheet to some good effect. It is important that the business plan is used as the engine room of the whole project. It will provide very important pointers as to the likely revenues and to the equally important costs. It trumpets to all the rewards if the product succeeds, and indicates the need for actions to deliver the numbers in the plan.

Most companies are motivated by profits, and clearly no company can afford to stand still with regard to the production of new products. The replacement of existing products with better, more cost-effective replacements is a continuing process. This may mean no changes in selling prices, or even functionality, but it could mean more efficient production by the use of new materials, or by producing the thing in a different way. It may also encourage customers to upgrade to a newer product, or to refocus attention to the new product from a competitor's product.

For example, an instrument maker may use a range of metal enclosures for his range of instruments, which would prove to be expensive even given the economies of scale. Switching to injection-moulded plastic cases, and at the same time the rationalisation of five different types to three new types, may provide major cost savings thus justifying the changes. The production of a few hundred cases per year of each type would be totally unacceptable when plastics injection moulding is used. There will come a point in the growth of the company when a critical mass will have been established, justifying the changeover. It may also allow the instrument maker to rationalise his products so that they all fit into a single plastic case, giving further cost savings. One of the key features in innovative companies is the ability of the team to think up new ideas. Another is to challenge some of the traditional thinking and 'industry practice' that may have been adequate for many years.

The business plan can be a very effective planning tool as well as a motivator to the higher echelons of the company with regard to future profits flow. The plan, however, must continue to grow with the project. It must essentially cover the whole project, not only in terms of direct costs, but also indirect costs, capital costs, and changeover costs, if one product is replacing another. In addition, the use of modern microcomputers allows the model to be fed with 'what if' scenarios, which give very important pointers as to how the project may develop into a business. Modern spreadsheets can be linked together so that the design of the business plan should be more on the lines of a business model. It is very helpful at an early stage if the logic of the system is worked out and understood. Most projects in a company will follow similar patterns and will also benefit if they report in the same way. However, smaller companies with limited resources and without the access to 'computer whizkids' can still buy 'off the shelf' business plans or development plans, which really are no more than 'macros' which run on a given make of spreadsheet. Some of these are available as public domain software, in both the IBM PC and the Unix market. Whilst not providing a strictly tailor-made product they do provide very good modules that are of benefit to most smaller companies and which do not deflect the team's time and energy into non-essential activities.

If a new product is expected to replace an existing product, in an existing market, and will also provide a new product in a different marketplace, then it is important that the forecasts are separated. Those forecasts should include volumes, margins, channel margins, etc., in the business plan. The reasons are obvious. The replacement of the existing product gives high degrees of success rating with the ability to forecast sales volumes and margins accurately, based upon very considerable past experience, trade contacts etc. With this new product in a different market, there is a completely different accuracy level with regard to volumes, margins and sales uptake.

When writing the plan, it is ideally written as two separate modules and the results consolidated into a forecast. If this is not possible, the other way is to have separate guesstimates of the sales volumes, margins and uptake, and then factorise them by a 'confidence factor'. However, while this is quite acceptable in earlier stages of the project, by pre-launch, it is hoped that work on the α and β tests would have been able to establish a more robust sales and production plan. By the pre-launch stage the figures should be as reliable as forecasting can make.

However, the argument for separate modules is a strong one. At the start of the project, with no guarantee of success, the temptation is to 'do with the minimum'. Later on, however, the business plan will have to deal with items like 'slower or faster uptake' or 'price attrition from competitor'. In these instances, when playing 'what if', the business model can be very quickly updated by simulating changes. In the above example, if the project is deemed to be under 'price attrition from competitors', this can be quickly simulated. Such simulations can quickly indicate to the marketing and production departments what degrees of freedom they have.

Marketing communications

Customers, distribution channels and sales forces, both internal and external, should be prepared for the launch, and training and seminars should be in progress. If relevant, appropriate PR, press briefings, etc. should be in progress. The product manager should be responsible for preparing and vetting the publicity material and this should not be delegated to the PR company, nor to the marketing manager or the marketing communications manager. The reason is that they are often not fully conversant and might make claims that are wrong and then are printed. Once published the damage is done! This aspect of the pre-launch is vital.

Delaying tactics

Companies such as IBM have been very good in the past at announcing a brief new product specification, well in advance of the launch, and in doing so are running a spoiling exercise against competitors. Companies naturally aim their products at the market leader's existing product range and many customers will delay a decision until full specifications of the new product have been announced before making a decision. This means that the new product gets a bigger slice of the decision cake than if no announcement was made, as some buying decisions would have been taken before the new product was launched.

Marketing should have produced a comprehensive set of sales literature, brochures and pricing systems so that all the sales and distribution sales staff are fully conversant. It is often a good idea to write to each sales person in the distribution teams to ensure that they receive the same PR kit as the press. This keeps them firmly in the picture, acting as a motivator, and ensures that accurate information is passed to the final customer.

Beta test sites

Marketing in conjunction with sales, distribution and the technical team will have selected the beta test site and testing will be under way. Informal contact will have been kept with the sites to monitor progress, unless technical support is necessary and normal for this type of product. If technical support is an integral part of the company's product range, then valuable contacts and information can be gained by proactive calling to the beta sites to gauge reaction and pick up on problems that are likely to surface in the field and may not necessarily be apparent in either the laboratory or during the α test phase. In fact, in technical products, such work is valuable to understand how the product gets used by real customers in the field, rather than how the company thinks it is used. This specially applies when the product is used interactively with other third-party products. The building up of understanding of how the product works with third-party products is an important part of the beta test, and can be documented with an addendum to the installation guide. It can be a valuable sales aid, and confidence builder to distribution, sales outlets and the end user.

Strategic accounts

Beta tests can be used strategically to target large accounts. Sales staff in distribution always like to work on these large sites, because it enhances their reputations and allows them to meet major competition at large accounts with the knowledge that they have the manufacturer right behind them.

Research and development should have a comprehensive list of the beta test sites, a very clear idea of how they will analyse the results, and what technical support will be needed if necessary. If R&D staff are to be used to talk to customers as part of the β test programme, they should be well trained in talking to customers. This is because they tend to be very frank, and may well be critical of a competitor's product, which does not go down well with customers, specially when such criticism can be seen as to fault the buying decision. R&D staff also tend to be very blunt even with their own product, and its failings as they see them. They need to be very diplomatic and positive about their own product, and very mild in pointing out the shortcomings of competitors.

SITUATION 10

The MOD accepted that their Belgian FN rifle was inferior to the Russian Kalashnikov AK47, which has been made in its millions over the last 20 years. Its ordnance department produced a modern lightweight rifle, which proved to be fairly accurate, and relatively cheap to produce. Beta testing of the product was done by the Brigade of Guards, who had expressed reservations as to the use of the rifle in ceremonial guard duties and similar. They also tested it on firing ranges. It was introduced. Many armourers would not accept it.

The rifle was found to have severe loading problems in cold conditions and a tendency to jam in dusty and sandy conditions. Modifications cost the taxpayer £80m. Unlike most of its competitors, it could not be fired by lefthanders, eliminating 10–15 per cent of the serving forces, whose ability to fire left-handed was good, but whose ability to fire right-handed was mediocre or even poor. Introduced originally in 1982, it is on its sixth modification. It is still not considered to be as good as the AK47 which is over 30 years old.

Q1   *What sorts of tests should the rifle have been put to at the alpha test stages?*

Q2   *How would you arrange a comprehensive beta test to ensure that it is as good or better than the AK47?*

Q3   *If at the end of the beta tests the rifle still was not as good as the FN or AK47, what would you do then?*

11

STAGE 5 – BEFORE GATE 5:
Launch

CAUTIONARY TALE 11

A Japanese company virtually copied the intellectual rights of a US company and launched a printer that was 30 per cent cheaper than the patented US rival. It made inroads into the US company's market share and was met with 'class actions' in 52 different countries worldwide for patent infringement. The ensuing court case cost the company $180m in compensation, and had all its product stocks destroyed.

COMMENT

*The product failed **Right product**, as it was a copy of a rival's product, so much so that the two mechanisms were interchangeable. It was not a product ; it was a copy of another maker's patented technology. This was blatant copying and could not have fallen into the 'accidental' or 'parallel development' type of patent infringement which does occur. Such copying is very costly!*

GENERAL

The decision by the company to launch the product means that it expects the product to be a major revenue producer. It does not expect the product to suffer any 'showstoppers' or too much undue or unanticipated competition. If in a new market, the product will be supported by appropriate PR and advertising and support from the distribution channels.

Technical

The technical department by this stage will feel a bit deflated. Its major contribution will be winding down, and it should be encouraged to analyse results from the beta test and make proposals, where relevant, with regard to cost reductions. It may also have ideas on a next product down the line or a derivative version for a different or near related market.

Production

The production department will be working hard on improving the process, reducing quality problems, and building up stocks for the launch. Clearly, in fiscal products this will be in the way of supportive literature and in the case of service products a similar regime will apply. In heavy engineering the stock product will be the first machine. As the actual roll out plan will vary for each company and its products, so the actual sales versus budget figure will be different. Almost invariably, it is either well over, or under, the predicted figure. Production should have a set of alternative plans, so that it has worked out and rehearsed alternative production rates.

Marketing

Marketing will be very busy in a number of areas. It will be actively involved in the business plan and be responsible for pricing, sales forecasting, advertising, publicity and sales literature. It should also be looking at volume monitoring so that after initial launch it is able to alter the sales forecast on a weekly basis, until such time as experience allows longer periods of forecasting. After initial launch, there is always a 'lag phase' where things tend to suddenly go quiet. This is the best time to arrange for press reviews, informed industry comment, etc. to be published, so that there is a renewing of interest in the product and the company, and which considerably aids the distribution system to shift stocks. Marketing should also keep track of competitors' reactions specially with regard to price changes or 'spoiling tactics'.

In order to bridge the 'flat period' after launch, some products can be offered with special deals to enhance interest. Some capital products can be offered on 'evaluation lease' at special rates. Others can be tied into a deal with existing products. Special regional evaluation days can be set up so that selected invitees can see and use the product. Some products need to be 'pushed' in place of other rivals. Marketing departments should be actively working with sales to ensure that a competitor has not run special promotions to sell his product by making the product more attractive to sell. (Increased margins, special offers, incentives for distribution sales staff etc.) The best way of preventing this, is to put in place a promotion that pre-empts the opposition.

Sales

The sales team will be in its element. It has a new product with a good potential market. It has been involved in the alpha and beta test programmes, and is enthusiastic about the products and markets. It will be involved in motivating distribution and the salespeople and will also need to be acting as eyes and ears of the company in reporting both on this product and on the reaction of competition. Sales will need to work with marketing to ensure that there is an ongoing push, and that downturns in initial sales are due to normal events, and not problems with the product's distribution, or competitor activities.

Technical support

If the product requires technical support either by direct interaction with end users, sales teams, or the distributor's sales teams, then the department will be at its busiest. It should analyse the enquiries, and think of producing a simple leaflet or pamphlet in conjunction with marketing, giving answers to the top ten most frequent technical support problems. The same sort of system can work very well for both service-based products and financial products. Inevitably, salespeople, trade enquiries and end user enquiries will be routed to the technical support department, if sales cannot directly handle the question. Technical support should also be looking to improve the technical manuals of the product, in light of its experiences. With products that interact with third-party products, brief technical sheets that explain how the products interact, and to get them working, can be invaluable sales aids. They act as major confidence boosters, specially to the third-party distributors, whose personnel will not have been trained in the product.

SUCCESS STORY

For example, Printronix, a major supplier of computer-based printers, relied on its products being connected to third-party computer systems, such as DEC, Wang, IBM, ICL etc. It produced simple 'crib sheets' which told users and distributors how to connect to the host's system, which switches (180 different ones) to set, and how to make the computer recognise the printer. This meant that most systems could be up and running in ten minutes, rather than the hours necessary to read and understand the three manuals that were sent with the machine. It sold a lot of product.

Finance

Finance will still be working on the business plan, but elements will have been transferred to the budgeting process and the major problems will be one of forecasting, and cash flow. If selling in new channels or markets, there will be the inevitable problems with credit applications, unfamiliarity in the customer base and how the market does business. Order patterns again may be completely different from a more established product as many customers will be 'testing the water'.

Lessons

If you talk to any experienced company director, each new product launch produces a refinement to the previous launch. It is often a good idea, at some stage, to list the do's and dont's so that next time a different team will have some experience to fall back on. A post mortem is often well worth the effort. If the product has launched very differently from the predictions, it will be useful to identify why, so that when the next product is launched the same mistake is not made again. As an exercise, if you talk to core team members about the launch of their new product, they will have a short list of 'things they would do differently next time'.

Quality control

It is also a good idea to try a random sample of real customers, and to poll them on their purchase, with regard to the 'quality of the sale' . This measures how the product was sold to them and whether it met their expectations, and if not why not. In retail-type products, often the customer's expectation is sadly lower than it should be. How many video recorders are lying under-used, in old peoples' households, simply because they are too complicated for them to understand, or use? In a competitive situation, understanding the 'quality of the sale' may give the product a competitive advantage. This advantage may be repeatable for other products or follow-on products. What a distributor says he does, and actually does, may affect the product's saleability. Understanding the shortcomings may well allow the selling process and emphasis, to change.

Market research

Let us look at the case of a Korean microwave manufacturer, which designed a small oven for caravan and holiday use. It was overwhelmed with orders, simply because it was ideal for single people, or for cooking small quantities of food. Its major benefit was that it had a simple on/off switch and a timer. It was easy to use and 95 per cent of all sales were in conventional households that preferred the product over the bigger and more sophisticated rivals. Regretfully, the Korean company did not instigate any market research as to why customers were buying their products. Had it done so, it would have been able to produce a range of products which would have taken a much larger share of the market.

SUCCESS STORY

In another case, the manufacturer of 'fluorescent light bulbs' trained his distributors' sales forces to emphasise the cost and energy savings of the product compared with conventional light bulbs. This was fine for conventional domestic households, but a random sample of industrial customers revealed that they had another motive. They wanted a longer lasting product because of the cost of replacing bulbs in very difficult and inaccessible conditions. The bulb lasted 15 times longer than normal, which dramatically reduced the frequency of maintenance. The sales pitch was changed to stress both the cost savings and the frequency of maintenance. The product is now the market leader in industrial applications.

Product variance

Once a product has been launched there are possibilities for part number changes that can be supported by BS5750 or ISO 9000. These may be cosmetic changes to the product such as 'badge engineering' or the production of a version for a particular customer. It may also be for a specific market, so that the changes are say, in documentation, power supply (e.g. 110 v) or even minor changes to meet country regulations (VDE or FDA). For example, certain food additives can be sold in the EC and are banned in US and other countries.

CASE STUDY

More detailed changes may need to be subject to stringent testing, putting the product back to Stage 4 (Pre-launch) in the New Products Scheme to ensure adequate β testing. Centronics Inc., a major computer peripherals maker, launched products designed in US for use in Europe with a 220 volt supply. No testing was done in Europe prior to shipping because their product was working well in 110 volt markets. When launched, the product worked erratically in some countries but not in others. Subsequent investigation revealed that the power supply worked in countries with 220 volt supplies, but where 240 volts was normal, such as the UK and Germany, the system broke down. The product quickly got a reputation for unreliability and even though the faults were correctly rectified, it never came near to its sales potential in Europe.

Learning from the market

Many products will be used for a variety of different end user applications, or in conjunction with other products. Inevitably some problems will surface, which could not reasonably be predicted by the α and β test. This means that some product redesign may be needed. The core team may want to launch the redesigned product as a 'follow-on product'. Some marketeers are very clever at introducing 'product upgrades' which are little more than the previous version with a few minor problems solved. In other situations, there may be nothing wrong with the product, but if that product is expected to work with a whole range of third-party products, then a short experience addendum can be published. In essence this is an instillation of experience from the field.

SUCCESS STORY

A lawnmower maker launched a product in the US where many localities required the engine to run exclusively on unleaded fuel. They provided a simple addendum, which indicated a different type of spark plug, and simple instructions as how to set the carburettor for unleaded fuel. This meant that a buyer of their product, required to use unleaded fuel, could conform to local conditions.

If the product is technical, and requires the support of a technical support system, the instillation of the most popular problems into a set of field experience notes will dramatically reduce the workload on the support service. Most customers will actually welcome a photocopied update to the original technical literature, as it clearly indicates the willingness of the company to make the product as easy as possible to install.

SITUATION

Your role: You are a company director.

The company has used Dither and Scrattchet, Patent Agents for many years. During the development of your new hover lawnmower it has a good consumer reaction. The production is ready to go for volume, and it has a good order book. Patent agents, Dither and Scrattchet, have done various searches, and have assured the company that the design does not contravene any patents, or industrial designs.

During the launch, however, as a bombshell, the company has been advised that Mr Scrattchet had a personal problem and has unfortunately overlooked a patent. That being so, it would appear that the company would be infringing a valid patent by selling the product.

Q? *What do you do now?*

12

GETTING IT RIGHT
Some Successful Product Stories

APV – *novel food processing*

BJ Garden Furniture – *novel wooden furniture with appeal*

Psion – *leading edge of the hand-held computer business*

EDC – *developing a large diving operation in three years*

JCB – *producing a novel JCB product using electronics*

Digilock – *novel anti-theft devices for vehicles.*

APV BAKER

(Part of the APV Group)

Background

Aluminium Plant and Vessel is a long-established company expert in the processing of food products. Since its inception APV has embraced many technologies and has merged with companies such as Baker Perkins and Burnett & Rolfe, to produce one of the world's larger companies specialising in food and drink processing. Traditional methods of preserving foods obviously includes salting, drying, pickling, freezing, and heating to kill off or attenuate the growth of harmful bacteria.

Effects of preservation processes

Looking at the area of heating of food products there are methods that have existed for centuries, involving heating in a vessel, in a can, or even autoclaving. Each method has its advantages and disadvantages. Louis Pasteur discovered the idea of heating milk to such a temperature as to kill certain bacilli that caused tuberculosis, but which did not substantially alter the taste of the product. Heating and freezing of the food results in subtle flavour changes in most foodstuffs, and in many there is a substantial change in the texture of the product. Strawberries are an example in question. Heat or freeze them, and you end up with a fruit that tastes of strawberries but which is 'mushy' due to the breakdown of the cell walls. Raspberries fare much better in the same tests, but even then it is clear to a consumer which fruit is fresh and which has been preserved. Pasteurisation of liquids is a viable proposition, while autoclaving of canned meat products is a standard technique. However the two processes cannot be changed with the substrates. Autoclaved milk would be a disaster.

Innovation

The passage of a current directly through the food has been known about and postulated since the 1880s. However, little success has been achieved in research laboratories but the process was seen to have important advantages. They are shorter exposure times to heat, resulting in less damage to the food product, and higher solids' ratios.

In 1975, EA Technology Ltd started experimenting with a new type of in-line heating element, which allows current to be passed directly through the foodstuff thus sterilising it. By 1980 it had progressed to such an extent that it was able to demonstrate in the lab a system that was reliable. In that year, the Technical Director of APV visited the company during an open day, and realised that it possibly had solved the problem. In any event, it was farther ahead than APV itself. The upshot was that APV licensed the patents filed by EA Technology, and developed the process, based on its own extensive knowledge of the food processing market.

At this stage, this was a very good move. APV could provide a world-wide customer base, and the credibility of a major player, and the experience of building and testing new food processing plant. (All of which EA Technology lacked.) From EA Technology's point of view its partner provided the marketing and customer base, and the experience of producing the equipment, while it contributed the key heating element that ensured a reliable process. A classic case of co-operation to achieve a successful outcome for both companies. However, the processes took some years to engineer, develop and get approved. The process is called ohmic heating, and requires a number of in-line elements, such that the current is pumped at uniform rate and the entire volume of foodstuff is sterilised. A considerable amount of time was spent in ensuring that there is uniform current transfer, and that there are no 'hot spots' or areas where the food remains unsterilised.

By 1982, APV Baker has convinced itself that it has a viable application process. However in such situations, the entire viability of the project was not simply a matter of scaling up the size of the plant. It was dependent on several other parties who had key components. Apart from EA Technology and its current-transferring elements, a specialist pump supplier was needed, and downstream collaborators. There is no point in providing a sterile food product if you cannot pack it in sterile containers for onward sale.

Once the food has been sterilised it needs to be filled into appropriate containers in completely sterile conditions. APV does not make filling systems so it needed to encourage and motivate manufacturers of filler systems to design plant that could be mated with the ohmic heating system to provide a filling line. Without such co-operation the project would not have proceeded. Typically a complete system would cost £5–7m, so the degree of commitment and co-operation was vital. As in any co-operative venture, where several manufacturers are creating a solution to problem, there are numerous benefits in cross recommendation. Thus the sale of a plant would result in the sale of specialist pumps, and a filling line, which would not have been sold, except 'on the back of' the ohmic process.

Even with the correct components in place other major hurdles that needed to be overcome were the conservatism of the food industry and the need to convince the food regulatory authorities that the process was safe, reliable and consistent. Such work took two years and involved developing microbiological techniques to monitor and check the foodstuff before and after the heating process. So much so, deliberately contaminated foods were treated and the process monitored.

Development

The process had been started in 1975 by EA Technology and by 1985 engineering had largely been completed, collaborative suppliers had been brought on board, and comprehensive testing was under way. APV's main board was supportive and in view of the costs involved it needed to be! The project was managing itself well, and was ensuring that it was evangelising its rate of progress, so that all parts of the company were aware of what it was doing, and crucially the board of directors was behind the project and looking at the vision of the new process. This vision was that the process could provide a much more rapid and productive method of food sterilisation, with better taste and texture capability, and therefore able to enter into key niche markets as a driver to wider acceptability as a process. In the longer term, the vision was that about 10 per cent of the world's food could be processed by this new technology, and this would provide a long-term revenue stream and a business that could be defined as having a competitive edge. Between 1987 and 1988, extensive microbiological tests were done and submitted to the Advisory Committee on Foods for approval. Its own suggestions resulted in further testing using deliberately contaminated food. Also a standard needed to be devised with regard to electrical safety. As such a process did not exist before, the Electrical Research Association at Leatherhead devised standards which were essential to the safety of the plant operators.

In 1988 APV managed to sell its first two systems to the Far East. These were significant in that it convinced its customers of the viability and efficiency of the process and gave the customers the ability to provide fresher tasting product, with better texture, giving them a competitive edge in their own markets and allowing them to launch food products which were differentiated from the competition. For example, one yoghurt maker was able to produce fruit yoghurt using whole fruit rather than macerated pieces of fruit. This looked and tasted as if the fresh fruit had just been put into the yoghurt, and gave it the differentiation in the market which resulted in increased market share.

Year of reckoning

Having had a reasonably successful start to the commercial launch of the project, it still had other major hurdles to jump. US Food and Drug Administration approvals were required in the US market, which is the largest of the worldwide markets. Each prospective customer and specific food needs approval and extensive testing by the customers to provide the body of information to satisfy the FDA. In addition all components, including the downstream filler system, also need approvals for the materials of construction. Hence, such approval was the key to opening up the US markets, and such approval is widely accepted in other parts of the world and becomes a 'lead specification'. Such specifications are important because once granted they give an aura of approval to any food producer, which may have to satisfy local food regulations which are extremely unlikely to be as rigorous the FDA approval system.

In 1989, APV sold no ohmic processing systems. Clearly this was a setback and while FDA approval had not yet been sought, it had been hoped to sell into other areas of the world. Shareholders were typical in that they were asking for short-term profits, and there must have been strong pressures on the APV board, which was investing a lot of time and money in the project. Regretfully short termism is a problem with many Western companies, which are expected, by the City and the shareholders, to produce near instant results,.

The core development team had produced three different business plans that looked at low growth, medium growth and high growth. These helped to steady the resolve of the company in backing the long-term view. In addition it was decided that a portable plant was needed to be able to let customers test the process themselves, rather than to rely on short-term visits to the plant in Crawley in Sussex. The APV board sanctioned the building of two small 'test plants' which were to be leased to prospective customers so that they could do evaluation in house testing. In so doing, they could convince themselves of the advantages of the process, in terms of throughput, quality of the product, and efficiency of sterilisation. Two plants were built, and fairly quickly sold, as lease customers soon became 'buy' customers.

This 'puppy dog selling' technique is an expensive option for any capital intensive supplier. On the other hand it indicates the commitment to the process by the company and the confidence that it has in its product. The facility for a customer to set up and run, and then to produce and test consistent product, is vital in any new business. The customer then becomes the product's best sales representative, and will evangelise the process within his company. In some marketplaces, 'puppy dog selling' is not needed as the customer will be quite happy to show other prospective customers his working system. However, in the case of APV, each food supplier jealously guards its process and identity, so that third-party referral is not possible. In this case, the idea of evaluation plant is a good one, and in the case of a new process in a conservative industry is a key 'seeder' of the marketplace. In ten years' time when the new process is accepted and is widely installed, such a system would not be needed.

Approval

In 1991 APV obtained its first FDA approval and since then has had success in selling its product in the US markets. Further sales in the Far East have been made as have sales in Europe. Repeat sales have started, which means that a small plant has been producing product, and is either to be replaced by a larger one, or the experience has led the customer to use the process on a new product. In any event it is an important indicator of customer confidence and satisfaction.

Break-even point

The vision of a much wider acceptance of the technology is slowly beginning to materialise. The project broke even in 1993, so that its investment from 1980 to 1993 is starting to produce fruit. Undoubtedly the process will gain popularity with time and a much wider range of foods will be processed in this way, so that the vision of 10 per cent of all food processing using the technology will be realised. If a figure anywhere near 10 per cent is achieved in the next 20 years, the project must be viewed as a huge success and will become a cash cow for decades to come. It is to be hoped that this will be of considerable comfort to the shareholders.

Competitor failures

As the concept is not patented, but the process and knowledge are, this gives APV a strong competitive edge for the decades to come. Two rival companies have attempted to launch similar products and failed and have withdrawn them. Key drivers in this project can be identified as:

1   The knowledge that ohmic heating produces faster processing of certain food types
2   The process causes less cellular damage, giving the customer food processor a better product

3 The process allows higher solids/liquids ratios than other rival processes, making the impossible, possible

4 The process was possible, consistent and produced sterile product

5 The process was tested and approved by worldwide health monitoring organisations

6 Key alliance of APV with pump and filler suppliers providing a complete food processing solution

7 Steady nerve and full support of APV board and ability to look long term

8 Customers tested the process and produced better product giving them a competitive edge in their market

9 Portable test plant increased customer confidence and allowed in-house and detailed evaluation

10 Worldwide penetration of niche markets, allowing expansion into a wider market base with time

11 Repeat orders indicating high levels of customer confidence

12 Availability of business plan, in which event met the medium-growth scenario.

Degree of risk

This project was a medium to high risk when started, as the process was completely new. However, as the initial R&D demonstrated the efficacy of the process, the risk was reduced. The important point was that the process was new, but the marketplace was known and APV was a leading player in that marketplace. However, crucial to the overall success were the statutory food approvals, without which the process would have been academic. On the other side the reward factors over the next few decades are high. Ohmic heating gives APV Baker an exclusive process, which provides several key customer benefits, not offered by other systems. This will give them sustainable, long-term points of difference in the world food processing market.

BJ GARDEN FURNITURE

Background

A small garden furniture company is the subject of this study. Barry East, the proprietor, was made redundant by PowerGen having worked his way up to power station superintendent. At the age of 53 it was considered unlikely that he would get another job. While unemployed he visited a garden show, and having an interest in woodwork and carpentry was very surprised to see both the pricing and quality of softwood garden furniture. Investigation at the local library produced a number of books on the subject, among them a Victorian book with some pictures of stone garden furniture. Barry felt that he could make the same basic designs in wood, modified to suit the smaller urban garden.

Prototype

He thought that he could produce in good-quality softwood, a two-seater garden bench, with a table arrangement in between, so that either seat could stand food and drink on the table, or use the table to work on. He built a prototype in the garage and showed it to friends, who liked the concept.

Testing the market

He took a very small pitch at a garden show in Kent, and sold six units during the day. He was surprised to get telephone calls from the organisers, who had enquiries from the public, and he sold another eight units retrospectively.

Customer reaction

In addition, the show allowed him to talk to the potential customers, who made comments about the height of the seat, and the provision of a hole in the unit to take a sunshade. One customer suggested a removable cushion arrangement, which was tried, and then implemented. Based on the customer reaction he modified the original prototype to have two alternative seat backs, and raised the height of the legs by 2 cm. A hole was provided for sunshade and a cushion arrangement made that allowed a single cushion which 'hinged' in the middle and attached to the seat back by an elastic strap. These options allowed the basic unit to be sold with options for both seat cushions and sunshades, which were made by outside companies but which could be sold at 150 per cent profit margins. The unit was called Tea for Two.

Establishing a business plan

At that stage, he decided to consult the author with regard to forming a simple business plan. He estimated that he could produce five different items, the Tea for Two garden bench, a garden chair with side table, picnic tables in two sizes and a normal garden bench. With modest sales of each he could provide a basic source of income and provide some outlet to assuage his boredom. Product analysis showed that with the right design he could source only two different sizes of timber. His competitors were using the lowest quality softwood with mediocre finish.

Points of difference

He decided that he could offer a number of points of difference. His innovative designs, high-quality softwood, and local service area.

He needed good softwood of a consistent quality. He spent several weeks examining different timber supply companies, and selected a company whose help was subsequently vital. In addition to providing a consistent source they also helped by shipping part loads because of space problems. As the furniture was designed to stay in the garden 12 months per year, a reliable preservative treatment was essential, and several different methods of wood preserving were tried, with a view to both wood preservation and colour preservation. He decided to differentiate his product in respect of both the designs and the quality of the timber. With regard to pricing he pitched his pricing between the low-cost softwood and the much higher cost hardwood. As the furniture had to be delivered complete, there was an obvious geographical limit to the delivery area, so that it was decided to limit sales to Kent and East Sussex, because the delivery cost became prohibitive. The business plan required a modest sale of 100 units (mixed) in the first year to cover show expenses, limited capital investment and provide a modest profit. He looked at profit margins and found that he could make 120 per cent in direct sales to the public but very low margins by selling via garden centres. It was decided to market directly to the public, as there was a limited production capacity.

Various shows were booked and the product range expanded to five items. Some interesting results indicated that the larger of the picnic tables had a direct appeal to public houses. It was robust and well built and he sold some to publicans who wanted to replace old picnic tables. This provided a useful source of income in the winter months, as publicans could be canvassed and the product made in the winter, so using up the slack period.

Local newspaper advertising was tried and found to be ineffective. Outside shows produced sales on the day and allowed interested parties to take away literature from which they subsequently bought. Many such items produced sales anything up to 12 months later.

Competitor analysis

Examination of competitors showed that the wood was inferior in quality, thickness and finish. Preservative treatments were either low-cost or completely absent. Fixings tended to be cadmium-plated steel screws which rusted after a year in the garden. No innovative designs were available. Barry decided to differentiate his product by quality, using brass screws, and providing innovative designs, and very good preservative treatments. In the latter part of the year, at the SE Garden Festival, he sold 31 Tea for Two units. Hardwood makers sold 3 hardwood benches, and the other softwood supplier sold only 11 three-seater bench units, even though there was a £35 price advantage. Brochure handouts produced another 20 orders for the Tea for Two after the show. This quality versus price decision was correct. The public clearly voted 3:1 to buy the higher priced Tea for Two rather than the lower priced softwood bench, and clearly the hardwood benches were so expensive that they were not an impulse buy. In the first year he sold 121 Tea for Two units, and lesser amounts of the other items, making total sales of 202 units. Investment was made into simple bandsaws, power screwdrivers and a more comprehensive brochure. In addition several prototype variants were produced. A version of the Tea for Two was produced, which would fit into a corner in a patio, and also one that allowed the seated occupants to view each other at 120 degrees.

Increasing sales

During the second year the orders started rolling in fast. Leaflets handed out the previous season were producing unexpected orders and third parties were placing orders for their own benches having seen and used those sold to friends. The newer prototypes were shown at garden shows early in the year and resulted in orders from old people's homes, and hospitals. The same show which gave orders of 6 units in the first year, produced 51 orders at the show for the Tea for Two, and 17 subsequent telephone orders immediately after. During the summer months the company is working 15 hours per day, and 7 days per week to meet demand. During the winter, the time is spent on new prototypes, building up 'kits' that can be quickly assembled at the start of the season. Filling the public house orders, and building special orders for picnic benches takes up much of the rest of the time.

At the end of the second year the company sold 782 of the Tea For Two units (and variants) with little change in investment in machinery. For the third year it is expected that the company will change its sales strategy of remaining local, and will conclude a deal to allow furniture to be transported complete on nationwide basis. If this takes place then there will need to be fundamental changes in sales literature, advertising, and show support, which will mean a larger and more focused workforce.

COMMENT

This company was started on less than £500 capital, and was reliant on low technology. The advantage of this approach was that prototypes could be built cheaply, and exhibited for customer comment. The simple modifications suggested by customers resulted in rapid improvement in the prototype and allowed for a downstream revenue stream to sell accessories.

Price versus quality was an issue. It was vital that the customer felt that he was getting good value for money, and the pitching of the prices above the lower cost softwood furniture was correct. Attempts to build the same furniture in hardwood were not successful, mainly because the prices required to provide the same margins took the furniture out of the 'impulse buy' category, in what was a major recession.

Innovative design was undoubtedly an important part. The Tea for Two became a magnet for persons walking around such shows, as they would stop to rest their legs for a few minutes. Quite a high proportion of casual sitters became customers, simply because they liked both the design and the comfort. Most were not even spoken to by a salesman.

Right Product *was met by the very positive customer response.*

Right Time *was met by the fact that such a unit had not been produced in wood before (at least not in Kent).*

Right Positioning *appears to be correct in that it is pitched in the middle cost band with good quality and competes with the cheaper softwood product and the expensive hardwood.*

Right Production is an issue. In year two they were stretched as the sales were nearly twice that predicted. More use must be made of the winter months, but the investment into 'kit' units requires high stocking levels. Production using semi-automation and an outside third party seems to be an option.

Right Price First-year prices were increased by 10 per cent in year two with a 600 per cent increase in sales. Clearly pricing was not an issue.

PSION
Doing it right

Background

Psion started life writing software for the defunct Sinclair computer range. In 1982 it pioneered the idea of producing a truly portable desktop organiser, and since that time has produced five major products with a number of variations. Several are still on sale (and doing good business) eight years after their initial launch.

Psion is a company in the forefront of the computer technology market, which at the moment is still a niche market. To a certain extent it is not assailed by the enormous demands for more speed and power, as its products still deliver most of the functions that 'real' computers do. In fact, market research statistics reveal that over 70 per cent of desktop computers are used for word processing, and 30 per cent for spreadsheets. Psion's offering has both spreadsheet and word processor built in, also database, organiser, etc. In fact, Psion provides most of the common type of programs used on the majority of computers in a hand-held format the size of a thick wallet. Unlike conventional computers they do not have disk drives to input and output data; they rely on solid state memory and chips to provide the same sort of functions as performed by disk drives. This is clearly well ahead of the desktop/laptop computer market, and gives it a competitive edge. The opportunity to license its expertise and know-how in other applications that do not conflict with its core operation is a second revenue producer.

Market segmentation

Early on in its development it identified two different markets – consumer and industrial. In the consumer market it still has three different products which account for 65 per cent of its overseas business. As there are differing levels of sophistication in these markets, older types of product still sell very well. For example the 1986 Mk 2 Organiser still sells at the rate of 5000 per month. No computer maker could claim that for its desktop products, as they have been superseded many times over. To a certain extent this is fashion. A 1986 desktop computer could do all the basic things expected of a 1995 desktop. Software is more demanding and has more functions. However, the need to electronically 'put pen to paper' is the same now as it was then. Hence, if an older design of Psion organiser offers the functions that the customer wants, at the right price, then a sale takes place. While this may partly be due to the nature of the niche market it is in, it may also be due to the advanced design of the unit which eight years later, is still not perceived to be out of date.

Industrial market

In the industrial market it found that it had to build fewer numbers of highly robust units for data collection and capture. These products were different, used for the collection of data and invariably to load into a larger computer for inventory or billing purposes. Meter reading and stock control being two typical functions; here, robustness and ease of use, with a single programme (tailor-made) are the order of the day.

Right product architecture

Luckily, earlier in the company's history it established a specification and an electronic structure that has stood its in very good stead for future requested products and applications which were not envisaged when the system was designed. The systems have no moving parts, therefore all programs have to be programmed and stored in silicon. This concept is absolutely suited to rugged industrial environments since the weakest link in notebook-type computers is the magnetic disk drives which are prone to damage due to vibration and are very badly affected by magnetic fields in industrial applications.

Establishing a new product

New product development is seen to be the life blood of the company. So much so that the board of directors remains intimately involved in the development of any new product. Put simply, it insists that every new product is a success, as the company cannot afford to fail in this marketplace.

Each new product is devised by a tightly knit team which is multidisciplinary. The base team is small in size and consists of marketing, electronics, R&D, software and production members. An outline business plan is used to drive the project. The team reports to the board of directors which acts as judge and jury. Psion, by its own admission, has regarded product development as being so crucial that it has not delegated responsibility to middle management. Jealously guarding the judge and jury function to themselves, the directors freely admit that every other function is devolved to middle management. Not so product development as they attach so much importance to it.

Development times

The product development times are about a year, which in computer terms is a long time but they have a much longer product life than normal desktop computers. In house prototypes are developed and much of the development of new features is tried out on non-technical staff to establish the acceptability of a product feature. Psion gets about 3000 calls a week on its free technical support line, and carefully monitors the types and reasons for the calls. In this way it is able to understand the users of its products, and is quick to understand the problems that exist with small keyboards and limited numbers of keys. In this way the potential new product is specified, and the hardware built. Software is added not only in house but externally and the normal beta test is done, largely by software developers and collaborators, who tend to find any problems much earlier than a field test would do, simply because the products are used intensively during the development and testing of the software.

Psion fully admits that as products get more sophisticated, it may have to rely more on 'focus group' activity and there is only so much that can be crammed into a wallet-sized unit. Often a decision needs to be made as to what to include and what not to include. Focus groups can give important pointers to the perceived usefulness of a new feature relative to another feature and this may overrule the view of the benevolent dictators who appoint themselves as judge and jury.

Potential new products

Currently they have four potential new products and about 80 R&D workers. Four separate teams are working on the four potential new products. In addition, it is becoming recognised that the architecture that Psion developed in the early 1980s is relevant to the embedding into other devices such as photocopiers, laser printers and probably a lot of future products that may end up on the 'IT superhighway' as part of a consumer product used in the home. Its ability to work with miniature devices which are solid state actually puts them in a large potential market and their experience (12 years longer than almost anyone else) makes then an ideal partner for future generations of products to be fitted to the much-vaunted optical fibre IT superhighways.

COMMENT

The Psion range meets the following critical criteria:

Right Product *It has sold 1.5m units in the consumer market, and many products bridge several generations of desktop computer.*

Right Position *Psion has remained a niche market player, and has built up an enviable reputation in sub-minature computers, both in the consumer market and in industrial markets. It exports 65 per cent of its consumer products. Its knowledge of solid state sub-miniature computing is marketable to other companies.*

Right Time *To a certain extent timing is a problem. It has launched a product range which is far ahead of normal state-of-the-art computers. In fact, if expansion to the consumer IT superhighway takes place with experience of the niche markets, then Psion has got it exactly right.*

Right Production *The company fulfils all its orders within normal time scales.*

Right Price *Pricing of the product in the consumer markets is key. If too low the margins suffer, which reduces R&D spend for the next product. If too high, the customers wont buy it. Psion has the pricing right.*

EUROPEAN DIVING CENTRE
Fethiye, Turkey

Background

This is a study of a service-based business started in strange conditions. Two of the partners are Welsh (uncle and nephew) and the third is Turkish. They met when the Turkish partner ran over one of the Welsh ones in Fethiye in Turkey four years ago. One Welsh partner was an experienced diver and he obtained a job teaching new divers on behalf of a local Turkish diving school. Having been an instructor in the army, he made various suggestions to his employers as to how to improve the quality of the courses offered to holidaymakers. This was not accepted and the low standards of safety and time-keeping were causing problems with largely British holidaymakers who were its client base. Turkish diving companies offered one-day trial dives and this formed the bulk of its limited business. No attempt was made to attract qualified sports divers and little advertising was used. Boats were of low quality.

Frustration

The three partners therefore decided that they could do better. They faced a major problem of how to communicate with their client base who were largely on one- or two-week package tours. Fethiye has some of the most interesting and equitable diving in the whole Mediterranean sea and so they formulated a service strategy which was based on:

1 Only British qualified divers would be used as instructors
2 Very high standards of safety with one instructor to every two novice divers
3 Latest diving sets and highest quality air compressor
4 Summer and winter diving
5 Direct advertising in Britain for sports diving and diving courses for novices
6 Local signboard and hotel advertising including pool demonstrations
7 High-quality boat.

Novel communication strategy

In order to attract the rapidly expanding British holiday population they devised the hotel demonstration dive. Most hotels and pensions in the Fethiye area had their own pools so the concept of a simple demonstration dive followed by potential clients being able to try the diving set in the pool resulted in a very high level of interest which could be converted to a trial dive at sea. In the first year (1991) they achieved about 2000 dives over the season. By chance, the boat which they chartered was large by diving standards, so they were able to offer relatives of the divers to come as well, providing a second revenue stream with no costs apart from lunch. In fact their pricing was lower than the cheapest boat trip but was every bit as good. Their initial budget indicated that to make a profit in the first year they would have to sell about 900 dives. However the combination of divers and non-divers made the first year more profitable than expected.

Defining workloads

It was quickly decided that one partner would devote his time to sales and promotion activities, the second would control the diving operations themselves, and the Turkish partner would spend her time on very considerable bureaucracy and administration. In fact the Anglo-Turkish element was to prove to be a winner, as several attempts were made to put the company out of business by the use of bureaucratic means. In the next year they found that they were getting repeat business from the previous year's client base and that they were getting requests for diving courses and winter diving trips. Water temperatures in the depths of winter are still higher than N. Europe in the height of summer and this provided a second market. This market was to provide a boat, support services, local knowledge hotel accommodation etc., for both clubs and individuals in the winter months. None of the Turkish diving schools did this.

1992 results

In 1992 the European Diving Centre achieved about 3500 dives and of this about 20 per cent were with qualified sports divers, and 15 per cent were for a course to convert novices into qualified sports divers. They purchased their first dive boat which they had leased for the first year.

1993 results

In 1993 they purchased a second boat for experienced divers, and their product mix was 30 per cent experienced dives, 20 per cent courses, and 50 per cent new trial dives. They sold about 8000 dives. They attended their first UK divers' show, and started package tours from the UK with specific dives in mind for both summer and winter diving. In addition they started magazine advertising in two different UK diving magazines with very good results. In 1993 they opened the first British Sub-Aqua Club-approved training school in Turkey.

Changing the product mix

By 1994 they were by far the largest diving school in Turkey. They were expecting to sell 15,000 dives in the Fethiye area and the anticipated product mix was 50 per cent novice and 50 per cent experienced divers. Much of their business is repeat business. They arrange clubs' tours, and about 50 per cent of all their business is generated in the UK, the rest locally in the Fethiye area; 50 per cent of their local trial dives come from swimming pool demonstrations in hotels and they cover 38 hotels on a weekly basis.

In 1995 they expect to open a second centre in Turkey because they feel that their experienced divers want a change of venue having been to Fethiye for a couple of years. In 1995 they will be listed in the majority of package tour brochures and will be linking with one tour operator to provide out-of-season diving combined with a week in Istanbul. They will be attending two dives shows this winter and they expect to sell in excess of 20,000 dives in 1995.

COMMENT

The European Diving Centre was lucky in its core team. Each complemented the other and the Turkish partner was to prove vital in providing local knowledge and support, and to fight relentlessly against both the Turkish government bureaucracy and the envy of local Turkish diving companies. Without the local partner they would have failed.

They quickly were able to see that the key to success was to overcome the reluctance of the British holidaymaker by operating a truly high standard of professionalism and safety. The concept of the pool demo was unique. The idea of trying and using the diving set (try before you buy) was a major contribution to client confidence, and once potential clients have done a few minutes in a pool they quickly see that they can do a more exciting dive in the sea. This concept alone rapidly increased novice divers, of which some 10 per cent decided they liked the sport and have taken up sports diving as a result. This means a regular and expanding client base who will spend money in the future in some of the best diving to be had in the Mediterranean.

Unlike their local Turkish rivals they got very well qualified to teach and certify diving qualifications for CMAS (French) PADI (USA) and BSAC (UK). In addition they realised that they had six months in winter with both sea temperatures and sunshine to promote Fethiye as a winter diving centre. They took strenuous steps to attract experienced divers from the UK. In 1994 they expected to sell more dives than the combined totals of six other diving schools in Fethiye and no doubt they did so.

Right Time *This is crucial. If they had set up any earlier they probably would not have the British client base. Had they done it much later they would have had much stiffer opposition from local schools.*

Right Product *Here the rapid expansion from novice dives to experienced and then into providing the complete services including accommodation and flights, meant that they were able to grow novices into regular clients.*

Right Production *As the services are limited, equipment and boats could be added without major capital costs of delay.*

Right Positioning *Here the British market was specifically catered for. They have aimed higher than the competition, both in quality and service, and in doing so are able to create additional revenues from peripheral activities. They have been able to exclude their competition by gaining much of their customer base in the UK and not locally.*

Right Pricing *As the Turkish lira is suffering over 70 per cent inflation, their pricing is largely done in sterling. This gives them considerable advantages compared to their competitors, as they can buy local services at the local rate, as and when required. They can compete on price with their competitors, while offering newer and better equipment, and higher safety standards.*

JCB
A new product for Scandinavia

Market-led design

JCB is extremely well known as a major manufacturer of digging and earth-moving equipment. Market research indicated a need to develop a new product specifically for the Scandinavian marketplace which was driven specifically by customer need.

This was a classic design of a product assembled to meet worse case conditions, on the basis that if it worked in Scandinavian markets it would work well in European and other markets. In the new product scheme it is suggested that design or testing of product should be done with 'worst case scenarios', in order to avoid duplication of effort. The marketplace was typified by harshness of climate, adverse terrain, shallow subsoils giving hard digging conditions, health and safety considerations, and high standards of cab comfort required for the extreme winter cold conditions.

Market research

Further market research and on-site consultations confirmed the outline specification and also that there were no competitor products (backhoe loaders) which met some or all of the above criteria. Many of the competitors' equipment were very large bulky machines with high capital and running costs.

In the late 1980s JCB decided to gain an increasing market share in Scandinavia by creating a product which met their needs and would provide valuable extra product in other markets. The market research indicated that the product would have to work in temperatures as low as −30 degrees Celsius, and was also tested at +40 degrees Celsius to ensure that the product would work in other markets at high temperatures. They implemented a design and development programme which lasted 18 months and cost about £250,000. Essentially this was the α test.

Market perceptions

In 1991 the market requirement was perceived to be for the machine to produce better traction in difficult terrain and improved manoeuvrability. Their JCB 4CX product was launched with four-wheel drive to increase traction and four-wheel steering to improve turning circle and ability to manoeuvre in tight spaces. This innovation allowed the product to behave like the competitor's articulated machines, but without the inherent thermodynamic instability associated with them. For the customer this meant a safer unit. As building sites and similar are notorious for safety violations and the lack of safety control, any product which is inherently safer has a competitive edge. The idea of using four equal-sized wheels rather than two large and two small, improved flotation on soft ground and must have also made the gearing considerably easier on both axles.

In 1992 it was discovered that the product needed better performance on steep gradients and better and easier gear changing. The response was an electronically controlled transmission system called Powershift. This allowed electronic selection of gears, speed and direction. Not dissimilar to a joystick on an aircraft, the operator can choose four forward and four reverse gears at the twist of a wrist. Speed of gear changing allows the machine's momentum to be maintained on gradients. The loader performance was changed so that the operator had to operate via a 'safety gate' which had three different positions. Feedback indicated that there was reduced operator fatigue, hence less chance of safety violations due to these innovative features.

Using innovative technology

Such a view was an important first for the company. Traditionally the JCB digger is a mechanical/hydraulic system which can be considered to be a mature 'low-tech' product. However, in order to accommodate the necessary features, it was clear that advanced electronics were needed. Nothing particularly special about that you might think.

Customer resistance?

However, advanced electronics has two enemies. Lack of understanding of the technologies and lack of acceptance within the marketplace. For example, would 'drive by wire' be accepted by an industry which was used to simple mechanical products. The following questions needed to be answered:

1 Would the industry accept electronic drive by wire rather than traditional hydraulics?
2 Would the electronics stand up to the rigorous and demanding field conditions – long term?
3 Would the electronics work over the temperature changes −30 to +40 degrees Celsius?
4 Would plant fitters be able to service and repair product in the field?
5 Would JCB be able to produce the same quality that its customers expected?
6 Could JCB produce advanced products using electronics and servo mechanisms?

Team approach

In response, JCB created a small team of marketing, engineering, manufacturing, R&D, and several key suppliers who were the basic engine behind the project.

Prototype

A simple prototype was built and tested in a variety of conditions. This was the only real α test sample. However, they were able to convince themselves that they could build a product which could meet customer needs and the fact that it was electronic could be 'sold' as part of the benefits package. When shown to customers, the reaction was enthusiastic. Customers wanted to try the product which was much smaller than the huge competitor vehicles used in the Scandinavian market. Field experience resulted in a number of changes to both the mechanical and electronics assemblies in light of that experience. The end result was that they satisfied items 2, 3, and 6. The rest would have to wait for further field trials during the β test.

β test

They built the first 50 machines and subjected them to a very thorough set of rigorous internal testing and disassembly to ensure that they were reliable and met item 5.

Items 1 and 4, could only be answered when the product had been sold. However, customer enthusiasm was high, so much so that they were invited to the UK to see their own machine being built at the factory. Most came!

Potential showstopper

However, it was not all plain sailing. The concept of a seat which revolved through 180 degrees, and in so doing activated one set of controls and deactivated the other, was apparently novel. However, on searching the patent literature, it was found to have been patented by another company. That in itself was not too serious except the other company was in the same sort of business! At this stage this could have been a serious showstopper but JCB were able, via patent agents, to demonstrate that the patent was actually not novel, as historically, a similar system had been demonstrated and thus was 'prior art'. This is a classic situation of where a company and its designers come up with what is a novel idea to them, and then find that someone else quite independently thought it up first.

The lessons to be learned are that a patented idea is a very good way of protecting a product idea and is worth the hassle and expense. The second lesson is that any novel idea needs to be screened early to check if it is patentable, or indeed if it is conflicting with a patented idea. Such screening or patent searching is not expensive, and can ideally be part of a Gate 1 review, so that any problems in that area are flagged and understood. In the case above, if the patent was not held by a competitor, the obvious course of action would be to license it, as this is quicker and probably less costly than a protracted court case. If it is held by a competitor, then licensing may well still be order; in some industries such as chemical and pharmaceutical, this is standard practice. Finally, if all else fails then the alternatives are either to design the product another way, or to prove 'prior art'. In any event, the earlier the problem is identified, the better and cheaper are the options. Showstoppers are expensive!

The second problem which came up was that JCB were not used to the requirements of electronic manufacture, simply because they had not been involved before. Most countries insist on the testing of electronic products to ensure that they do not inadvertently emit radio and magnetic radiation, which can interfere with other products, such as emergency radios, cellular telephones, radio and television broadcasts. This testing is quite time-consuming, and also quite costly. This aspect was a surprise the first time round, and the follow-on products in this range will have timescales built in to them, to allow for the testing against EMI. There are 'good practices' which ensure reduced EMI, and these need to be learned both from a production basis and from a design basis. As with any new branch of technology, the increase in the learning curve will take some time.

Improved control unit

In 1993 it was decided that easier control was needed with more comfort for the operator, who could easily be confined to the cab for up to ten hours, driving and operating the unit. JCB launched Servoplus which is a double command control unit. This gives him complete control over both the loader bucket and the excavator from two alternative positions and the ability to drive and steer the excavator. For working one site, the joystick controls replace the steering wheel, via an electronic system on the 'drive by wire basis'. For road use the conventional steering wheel is used. It was found that in field use, the digging of trenches is a time-consuming affair.

The excavator needs to be positioned astride the trench, the bucket used to dig a small portion of the trench. And then the need to 'up sticks' and move the machine some three metres to the next digging position and so on. The onset of Servoplus made the whole operation much quicker and smoother. The fully adjustable armrests contain the control pods which control the processes. Whenever the driver's seat is rotated, they are deactivated and the opposite set activated. This is miles away from the original JCB product which was a conventional farm tractor with a hydraulic bucket assembly.

The original design specifications have been provided and the product is a success in the Scandinavian market. The concept of 'drive by wire' is also a success, and customer and driver response indicates improved visibility while digging, increased floor space and a better operating environment with better cab conditions. Safety is also improved by reducing driver fatigue. The product has sold well in other markets, and its market share will undoubtedly expand.

Lessons learned

The JCB company was in a classic marketing situation. It had an existing product range and it knew from customer feedback that it could not totally fulfil the needs of the Scandinavian market. In order to fulfil those needs it needed a new product, which actually needed electronics to provide the degree of functionality required. From a market exposure point of view, it needed to launch a new product in a relatively unknown market, but where the name of JCB was known from other products sold into that market. This would be of a medium risk exposure.

Risk versus reward

What was undoubtedly a higher risk was the concept of using electronics to replace more conventional means. First, there was the implementation of the technology and second, and possibly more important, was the reaction of what is a conservative market, that had, for many years, been used to simple hydraulics. As it happened, the need to produce a product for the market resulted in unorthodox solutions which, because they satisfied the need and provided a solution, were not regarded as being that unorthodox. Thus the product became established and successful in that market, thus providing a springboard to other markets.

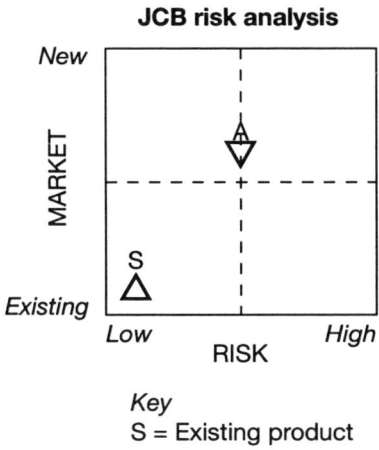

JCB risk analysis

Key
S = Existing product
A = New JCB 4CX

As with any new innovation, the learning curve was different to that which existed before. New ideas, methods, and means of working were required and needed to be implemented in production. This is not an easy matter, however well trained the workforce is, or how willing. However, this is one of the prices which have to be paid for innovation.

The important points which come out of the 4CX project are that:

1 Customers value the product more than the technology which it uses. Market share went from 14 to 25 per cent
2 JCB managed to launch a successful new product which used new techniques giving them a competitive edge
3 JCB managed to produce in volume on their plant a product using substantial electronics/hydraulic interaction
4 Their first product in this area will undoubtedly lead to others
5 Next time it will be easier due to the experience of building this first new product
6 Their design teams can consider new innovations which were not possible using conventional hydraulics
7 The product arrived on time, in budget, offering the features necessary to capture market share, or create a new market.

DIGILOCK – VEHICLE IMMOBILISATION HISTORY SPAN

Complete history of a medium-sized company using the NPS. Timescale from inception to product launch was seven months.

Trigger to innovation

David is a middle-aged electronics engineer working for a medium-sized company in the electronics industry. His wife's fairly elderly Rover Metro was stolen from outside the house in a classic pattern of joyriding. The car was found two days later, having been subjected to two broken windows, broken steering lock and damaged wiring loom. The costs to repair the vehicle were close to £500.

David was incensed to find that in addition to the inconvenience of the loss of the vehicle, his insurance premium would rise by 48 per cent as a result of his claim. In work, a casual discussion of his problem resulted in the idea of fitting an electronic switch as a solid state device inside either the ignition coil, or perhaps a solenoid (such as the starter motor) to prevent theft. An old ignition coil was dissected, and found to be suitable for modification and within days a working prototype was produced.

In the meantime, the insurance assessor had viewed the car and turned out to be one of David's old school friends. He revealed that most of his time was spent on car theft claims and that most cars were very easily stolen. This was now becoming a problem for the insurers, as some areas were very prone to car theft, and yet a few miles away it was virtually unknown. David mentioned his ideas and his friend gave him some insurance industry contacts.

Sanity check

David has the idea that they could produce a digital immobiliser and this would be a good volume product for his company for years to come. He found out the following:

1 Theft cost the insurance companies £1.2bn in 1993
2 Extra costs added another £1bn to clients (uninsured)
3 EC car theft is about £3bn/year
4 Most cars can be stolen in less than two minutes
5 Car alarms are widely ignored by the public
6 Simple immobilisers are the best anti-theft device

7 Two types of car theft 'recovered-damaged' (67 per cent) and 'permanent loss' (33 per cent)
8 His company could produce a unit for about £32 selling at about £90
9 His company had no direct experience of the automotive market
10 The potential market for the product was large
11 Patent searches revealed no prior art
12 They could not identify any direct competitor, though mechanical devices existed at lower prices.

He received broad support within the company and found that one member of marketing, Paul, was very interested in the idea, and was a natural partner.

Gate 1

David had made an outline proposal to his employers and they agreed to very limited time for both R&D and marketing to scope the project. David and Paul spent some time talking to the insurance companies.

Market research

Paul found a number of interesting items. Car thefts for the same models vary widely from area to area, which means that a learning process is involved, specially when joyriding is concerned. For example, a Rover Metro in Bristol was 100 times more likely to be stolen than in Bath 30 miles away. A Ford Escort on Tyneside was 80 times more likely to be stolen than in Portsmouth, with similar populations and inner city problems. In addition, insurance companies do not pool information so that there is no easy way of getting national figures. Several insurance companies were keen to encourage the fitting of immobilisers, by offering discounted premiums.

In Germany, it was impossible to get car insurance without a third-party immobiliser being fitted. (This was because thieves quickly work out how to bypass car manufacturers' offerings.)

Paul looked at commercial offerings. Most alarms were quite sophisticated, but widely ignored by the public. Most alarms had either no immobiliser or a very basic unit which cut off the ignition circuit and which could be quickly bypassed. Prices varied from £10 to over £700, with most 'electronic' systems costing over £120. There was no simple immobiliser system and when combined with alarms the lowest cost was about

£300. Mechanical devices locking the steering wheel or gear lever were quite effective.

In discussion with a crime protection officer, it was indicated that the more time-consuming the device to lock and unlock, the less likely it was to be used. Many cars were stolen with locks bought by the owner, but not fitted because 'I only left the car for five minutes'.

The insurance industry runs a series of standard tests and passing of those tests allows a device to be used to claim reduction on premiums. Some insurance companies have their own investigation and engineering departments, from whom valuable advice can be obtained.

Together they concocted a brief outline specification, which included the potential product, its suggested price, how and where it might be sold and how it differed from other products on the market. They 'took a view' as to the potential numbers which they might be able to sell over a five-year period. This was circulated around and the response varied from the enthusiastic to lukewarm. Some senior managers liked the idea, which departed from their core business of supplying electronic modules to other customers, and this gave better margins as it was close to the end user.

First attempt

R&D people had initially decided to use a keypad system which was cheap and would allow the system to retain several different 'PIN' numbers so that different drivers could use the car. They had produced a simple system which could unlock a system and was based on simple low-cost components. Their examination of the patent position suggested that there was nothing to prevent a patent being granted, so they filed a patent covering both ignition coils and solenoid coils. The essence of the patent was two separate electronic switches, which were incorporated inside the device. The first switch 'joined' the two halves of the coil together, so making it work. The second switch was an anti-tamper device and connected the coil windings to earth. If the second switch was not switched off first, it would result in the vehicle's fuses blowing as soon as current was applied. Their logic would handle this automatically in the electronics, but manual tampering would result in fuse blowing. In addition the system would run at a defined and secret voltage, which would switch on and off the embedded transistors. Most 'hot wiring' of cars relies on the car battery (12 volts) being used to bypass the security devices. In this event the low-voltage transistors would invoke the anti-tamper circuit automatically if the voltage was outside pre-determined limits. Such voltages would have to be generated by very specialist equipment, beyond the capabilities of most car thieves. As there were no clear competitors' devices that they could buy and analyse, they decided to build simple prototypes and test them.

MK 1 prototype

The first prototypes were built using manually modified ignition coils, and a simple keypad mounted on the dashboard. After six weeks the team interviewed every member who had driven the modified cars and the results were encouraging, but not brilliant. The salient features were:

1 The keypad was not liked, specially if the driving was short distance – frequent stop/start
2 The keypad took up a lot of 'dashboard real estate'
3 No two car makes have the same area available for the keypad
4 Tooling costs for aesthetically pleasing enclosure for the keypad were high
5 Keypad was insecure if the odd extra driver used the vehicle – specially in companies
6 PIN numbers got confused in near identical company cars with more than one driver
7 Circuit was prone to resetting itself with voltage spikes in field tests.
8 The rest of the circuit was reliable.

MK 2 prototype

The team divided its potential product into modules. Based on interaction with the insurance industry, whose certification system required more than one circuit protected, it established several modules:

1 Security system – unlocking system
2 Wiring loom
3 Protected circuit – coil, fuel, starter etc.

The system was proposed as either an ignition coil or fuel stop valve (or both). The security system was seen to be some sort of digital device which had a unique serial number that could be compared with serial numbers held within the system. Magnetic cards, barcodes, and similar were considered. It was assumed that the wiring loom was designed to be specific to the car and to the ignition coil fitted as part of the system.

Paul uncovered the fact that they had overlooked two other important markets. They were the diesel vehicle market and the boat market. In both these markets, there was predominance of diesel engines, which needed to have fuel stop valves fitted, as clearly they do not use ignition coils. Paul's work talking to the insurance companies (and a completely different sector) revealed that many thefts of diesel vans, lorries etc. were taking place, not for what they were, but for the loads that they were carrying. In addition the thefts of mechanical diggers, tractors, dumpers etc. was causing major concern, with the theft insurance costing £2000 per year on a £40,000 vehicle. In addition, hirers of such equipment lost major revenues when an item was stolen, because of the time taken to obtain the insurance money and the time to get a new vehicle delivered. In these cases the items were stolen by driving them away, at least far enough for them to be loaded onto a lorry. The key to theft prevention was to prevent the engine from working.

Boats on unattended moorings were another case of opportunism resulting in major insurance losses.

Development tests

A variety of different security locking devices were tried, including barcoded cards, magnetic access-type cards, infra-red cards. All were successful. Magnetic cards were deemed to be unsuitable due to the high magnetic flux in some conditions. However, talking to third parties revealed:

1 Comparatively high cost of card readers
2 Low long-term durability of the card
3 Comparatively high cost of building-in the product into the car dashboard.

One product that looked encouraging was a button device, similar in appearance to a watch battery. It could be touched onto a simple touch plate which decoded the serial number. This product was cheap, and meant that one touch plate system could be used for all vehicles and it only used up about 3 sq. cm and could be safely mounted on the steering column adjacent to the steering lock. It was known as a Touch memory.

Another product was found to be an RF tag system. This uses a very low-power radio signal which activates a small microchip on a keyfob or inside a keyfob assembly, then transmits its serial number to the radio receiver, which compares it with those built into the system. The advantage of this system was that the complete security system was transparent, and that the user would never know that a security system existed until the keyfob got lost! However the system would be more expensive.

The wiring loom should contain a very small microprocessor, embedded (to make it difficult to find) with the necessary fitting to connect to the vehicle's fuse box and the disabling devices coil, or solenoid etc.

The ignition coil system was a problem. Contacts with the major British maker resulted in a rebuff indicating that it had no interest in the venture. In the meantime, a range of solenoid-operated stop valves was identified, designed for automotive applications. The suppliers were very keen to co-operate. They could offer a range of products for connection in flexible rubber connections found on most cars and vans. For the bigger lorries, contractors' plant and boats, a larger valve could be connected to rigid pipe using industry standard compression connectors. These valves had been designed for built-in electronic indicators, and sufficient space was available to incorporate the additional semi-conductors defined in the patent.

Prototypes were built using both the touch memory and the RF tag security system, and unlocked fuel stop valves or modified ignition coils.

Gate 2

The insurance industry defined two basic types of car theft. The opportunistic joyride that could be prevented by a relatively simple immobiliser system, and the theft 'to order' which required a more complicated system which locked at least two different circuits.

The team realised that it had a product range which could be defined by price and by functionality. However, it needed funds to build and test several more prototypes, and at the same time to precisely define the product, and who would buy it, and how it would be sold. The company had no direct experience of the automotive market and hence it was somewhat of an unknown. It was assumed that the final sale price would be three times the manufactured price.

The team defined two products:

Low-cost product

Type	Security	Lock	Retail cost	Comment
Diesel	Touch memory	Fuel stop valve	£90	No endorsement
Petrol	Touch memory	Coil	£90	No endorsement

Medium-cost product

Type	Security	Lock	Retail cost	Comment
Diesel	RF tag	Fuel valve & starter	£200+	Insurers' endorsement
Petrol	RF tag	Coil & fuel stop valve	£200+	Insurers' endorsement

It needed to establish sales channels for:

1 Retail DIY retrofit
2 Trade retrofit
3 Mail order sales for DIY
4 Boat sales DIY/trade fitting
5 Fleet sales
6 Contractors' plant and equipment
7 Export to major EC countries
8 Possible insurance participation.

A number of other important parameters needed to be established:

1 Trade margins in different channels
2 Strategic partnerships – own label manufacture? A coil maker was a key partner.
3 Volume manufacture – savings and design features
4 Patent protection and trademarking
5 Thorough in-car testing by make and type
6 Understanding what could (and would) go wrong
7 Outline business plan with timing, costs and rewards
8 Testing of coil-based product with EMI testing
9 Establish suitable partner for coil making
10 Establish embedded solenoid coil for stop valve making.

The company made funds available for the project, but the project was at this time competing with two other projects for essentially a very limited budget both in terms of money and time. The company fully accepted that the rewards would be high and volumes large, but were also keenly aware that the automotive market was an unknown.

One R&D man was allocated for 50 per cent of his working time, and Paul from marketing spent 40 per cent of his time on establishing route to market and possible co-partners, both in terms of suppliers and co-sellers. Their action plan at Gate 2 was to identify and define the 'product' in its entirety, and to establish sales channels, and be able to produce the product in limited volumes for consumer testing

Gate 3

It was felt that some of the decisions that needed to be taken could be heavily influenced by the marketplace and so focus groups were set up to discuss the potential products. An independent chairman was appointed, who was a retired engineer but with fairly strong automotive connections. He set up five focus groups, which were based on:

1 Civil Service Motoring Association – general interest, mixed group
2 Ford Escort Owners club – Essex – specialist but run 'normal cars'
3 ANC Franchisees meeting – specialist diesel vans in commerce group
4 Brighton Mothers' Union meeting – women's perspective in major town
5 Specialist insurance focus group – buildings, car, household insurance focus discussion group.

Results

Two mock-up units were shown, which were working and briefly described. Panel members could try the unit for themselves. A number of interesting results came out of the work.

1 Most panel members were concerned that their cars would be stolen or broken into. Almost all knew a friend or relative who had suffered loss
2 Most would not attempt fitting the unit except some of the CSMA and Ford Escort group
3 Most liked the idea of the RF tag system. Pricing was considered to be on the high side if a straight purchase. It was considered to be good value if tied into some sort of discount on insurance costs
4 Almost all members thought that the low-cost system was good value. Many used mechanical anti-theft devices, and regarded them to be inconvenient and cumbersome

5 All groups did not care if the prime protection was the ignition coil, or fuel stop valve, or a combination
6 Some thought that the fitting of the system should be high profile with window stickers etc.
7 Almost all agreed that if they heard a car alarm they assumed it was a false alarm (due to wind etc.)
8 ANC group preferred the RF tag system as the vehicle was expected to stop/start during deliveries some 60 times per day. As the RF tag system would not involve any other actions the vehicle could be driven normally
9 The ANC group also stated that it would like to be able to 'change the locks' electronically.

The results from this test helped in the decision-making process.

Low cost

In the low-cost product for a start, there was little point from a manufacture or stocking point of view in having a whole range of products suitable for some 20 different ignition coils, for the cars that are on the British market, when a single fuel stop valve could achieve the same result. This meant a simpler range of products allied to the wiring loom (short, medium, long) and a single valve for all petrol and diesel cars and vans. For larger lorries and diggers etc. a larger stop valve could be supplied.

Medium cost

For the medium-cost system, where both coil and fuel stop valve would be used, the product would have to be car make specific. However, as the number of sales channels would be reduced this was not seen to be a major problem.

Freezing the product specification

Low cost

It was decided to freeze the product specification. The low-cost system would consist of two Touch memory buttons, with keyfob inserts, a Touch pad, to be sited near the steering lock, and a small light emitting diode assembly which turned from red to green when the security check had been completed. These two elements were connected to the wiring loom by 'idiot proof' plugs and the loom was passed under the dashboard and into the engine compartment, where it mated with a plug and socket into the stop valve, with flying leads to main fuse box assembly and earth.

No 'black box' would exist. The electronics would be embedded into the wiring loom.

Medium cost

The RF tag system would consist of the RF tag board which would be sited within the plastic housing round the steering column, mated with a wiring loom which passed under the dashboard, to emerge in the engine compartment, and connected to ignition coil (supplied), fuel stop valve and starter motor solenoid (supplied) and also to the main fuse box and earth connections.

Paul in R&D spent some time working on the various comments made at the focus groups. These were summarised as:

1 Loss of a set of keys including the Touch memory
2 Loss of RF tag
3 Effects of low voltages on the microprocessor
4 Stalling the car while driving
5 Being able to 'change the locks' electronically.

Loss of keys

It was quickly established that both the Touch memory and RF tag systems could be supplied as pre-numbered units which were unalterable, and 'read/write versions' which could be programmed with any serial number. As the loss of button or tags was inevitable, it was decided to program into the system a set of eight 'reserve' numbers which would be used so that spares could be produced. In order to avoid keeping records, the production system would automatically generate the numbers and feed them to an algorithm that would generate a unit serial number to be attached both by label and by secure wire tag. In the field, an owner would merely supply the unit serial number to generate new electronic keys, subject to the usual security checks. This meant an elegant solution to the problem and would allow the 'keys to be changed' when a car was sold. When a new and valid serial number button or tag was used, it would delete the previous number which had not been used for a period. This would stop the previous owner of the car using a 'spare set of keys' to take the car.

Vehicle hire problems

Contact with the plant hire and even the car/van hire market showed up another problem. A serious potential problem existed when a vehicle was sent out with two sets of keys and came back with only one. Such items as JCBs cost about £40,000 each, and go missing regularly, where they are driven away. When a set of keys is 'lost' are they really lost or is someone waiting for the right moment to steal the vehicle off site? Most vehicle hirers have many vehicles which look the same, and have a difficult job maintaining spare keys, without the extra problems of keyfobs containing RF tags or Touch memories.

It was proposed that in that market, the system would be supplied with master and slave capability. The microprocessor would recognise the master key and would then go into slave key mode. Up to three normal slave keys would be read by the system and logged into the microprocessor as being valid. The reallocation of the master would then end the process. Master keys were to be made using read/write buttons. These would contain a special security number unique to the hire company. Thus any master key could be used on any vehicle which would recognise the fleet security number.

When a vehicle was brought back with key loss, the existing slave keys would be put into a central reserve, after the master key was used to log-on new slave keys from the central reserve. This meant that in a couple of minutes the 'locks could be changed' without the need to maintain detailed records, other than ensuring that the master keys were safely locked away.

Software modifications

Software testing and validation took longer to implement this feature in this marketplace than in the rest of the systems put together.

Variable electrical conditions

David, taking on board concerns with regard to the product's reliability, decided that the product could easily be blamed for weaknesses in the car engine/battery/charging system which would be laid firmly at the product's door. If a car failed to start, then it 'must be the fault of the immobiliser'. In order to guard against this, the logic was changed so that the security check took place after the ignition circuit was switched on, but before the starter motor was used. The provision of the red/green light meant that the user would start the car on the green light. This in itself indicated that the system was working and security tests complete. At this point David decided to 'hand over' the operation of the transistors in fuel stop valve, ignition coil, or starter solenoid, to a separate circuit. This circuit was designed to operate with voltages as low as 3 volts and as high as 50 volts. It was provided with capacitors which maintained sufficient power to the transistors for 30 seconds in the event of a power glitch. In doing so it gave a clear indication of its operation via the green LED.

Production issues

Gurjit, a newish member of the production team, was seconded to the development team, so that the product could be electronically programmed in manufacture. Gurjit produced a validation program for an IBM PC, which was used in production without modification and is now used on a PC network as production has expanded. It was essential that production would be able to handle the programming of the microprocessor during the production of the products and to produce the necessary unit serial numbers via the special algorithm, which was controlled by the original numbers of the RF tag or Touch memory buttons.

Gurjit was also tasked with looking at the switch from a conventional microprocessor and individual components, to a single chip 'ASIC'. This is an application-specific integrated circuit and contains the entire circuit on one chip. There are large benefits in this approach. They are very cheap to make and test, and do not involve the testing of each component, as it is integrated. However, the downside is that once the full electronic circuit is laid down in silicon, the system cannot be altered. Typical cost savings were suggested as being about £7 per unit, in actual component cost, and a reduction in PCB size by 60 per cent. In addition, testing costs would reduce by about £1.20 per unit. Again, on the downside the design and validation costs would be about £10,000 and the equipment to program the units would cost about another £16,000.

The team considered these proposals and agreed that it was too early to consider switching. They had not conducted any detailed field testing as yet (β test), and they had no detailed information on the problems which may exist in the field after testing. As ASICs cannot be altered it was premature at this stage to consider their use. It would be appropriate after the launch of the products, and when full user experiences had been evaluated.

Gurjit had broken down the production stages into discrete items. Wiring looms as such would be made by a specialist and would consist of small, medium and long sizes for both the low-cost and medium-cost systems, which would be different. A specialist series of looms would be required for the lorry and plant hire markets, and for the boat market, a universal loom was postulated. One standard printed circuit board was to be made, and the only difference between low-cost, medium and the plant hire markets was the software programming. Such programming would be done on a 'campaign' basis. Ignition coils, stop valves and starter solenoids were to be supplied modified by the makers to the company's specifications. Touch memory buttons and RF tags, and the RF tag radio send/receive boards would be bought in from the makers. The Touch memory ports were to be made in house.

The team approached the company for more funds and a higher degree of commitment from almost all departments. The business plan was weak. There were no real efforts at sales forecasting. They needed greater experience of how the products would perform in the field. They needed to produce the products in a production environment and they needed to start looking at BS5750 procedures. The company agreed that the product looked good, it did not have any obvious competition in the UK, France and Germany, though there appeared to be a product in Italy which could be a rival.

Business plan

Sandra from accounts helped with a relatively simple business plan. Assuming a very modest roll out of the low-cost system with a follow on of the medium-cost system, the profits and cash flow looked good. Work identifying the various sales channels allowed realistic computer models of the various channels, and it was decided to select only three sales channels initially to gain experience. No export would be done in the first six months.

The board of directors sanctioned the spending of money in doing a comprehensive beta test, and the limited production of enough product to do the beta test and to have some working samples for third-party testing.

Gate 4

Beta test

Paul and Mary (from sales) had started to identify potential distributors both in the UK and in the EC. Showing of the same mock-ups as used for focus groups, generated a lot of enthusiasm. Margins were slightly higher than were predicted in Gate 1, so the retail pricing was increased to allow for the margins and for VAT. None of the distributors felt that the increase in price would affect sales, as there was no clear competitor at the time in terms of function or technology. The trade markets were very impressed at the concept of low component counts, which meant that they and their customers could keep stocks of modules and so mix and match to the end user need.

After pressure from the sales end, the team decided to set up and monitor a beta test based on selected sites which were brought from various distribution sales teams. This meant that the company could set up and monitor, in fairly closed conditions, the performance of the product as produced and tested.

Paul wrote a simple installation guide, which was designed for the DIY market. The guide was circulated internally and was found to lack appeal. It was agreed that photographs needed to be included. The team agreed that at this stage they could do the job themselves, but that for commercial launch a professional photographer would be needed. A set of different guides was made to include the low-cost system, the medium-cost and for lorry and plant hire markets. Simple white box packaging was arranged.

The team decided on a series of beta tests which were car specific. This included, for example, both carburettor version and fuel-injected models of such cars as the Ford Escort and the Vauxhall Cavalier. In all 150 samples in each category, low and medium cost would be tested, and 40 diesel lorries/diggers. The sales channels were able to identify fleet vehicles, where it was quite easy to fit and monitor the users.

Severe problem

Having set up the beta testing they placed the order, which was to make enough of the units in a trial production situation, and to assemble sufficient components. Having placed and had accepted their order for fuel stop valves, the bombshell arrived. The manufacturer of the in-line fuel stop valves had stopped production in Brazil. This was an important problem, as the key strategy was that considerably more systems used stop valves as ignition coils, and many used both. The stop valve maker was able to supply an alternative product, but it involved five discrete components, rather than the one integrated unit. This added about £3.50 to the unit pricing, or about £12 at retail.

The team worked hard on a solution. The new valve had a magnetically operated valve body which was a separate component to the coil that fitted to it. The coil in turn was connected to the wiring by a plug system. This entailed putting the transistors inside the plug unit, which needed to be screwed to the coil unit with a security screw to prevent tampering or by-passing. Even so it was a weak point. Discussion of the problem with the wiring loom supplier resulted in their sister company, which made both solenoid and transformers, contacting them. It could wind and integrate the transistors inside the coil and provide it in an epoxy-coated coil, which would be impossible to tamper with, and at costs which clawed back some of the price increases.

Changed sourcing

Samples were produced and proved to be highly effective. An initial order was fulfilled but the problems encountered proved to the team that they needed to gain the highest possible degree of control over the components and manufacture. The degree of security was actually higher than with the original stop valve, so all in all, the result was favourable.

Plant hire

An outside company approached the company with regard to the plant hire market. It sold specialist radio communications equipment which was retrofitted to larger items of plant hire equipment. It had had some problems with theft of equipment (along with the machine itself). It had heard from its insurers that the company had a good immobiliser system. It offered the company the possibility of being able to fit the immobiliser as part of its expanding product range. It was given an evaluation system with a larger fuel stop valve for the plant hire/lorry market. It was fitted to a vehicle in Exeter as part of a fleet. Within a week an attempt was made to steal the vehicle off a building site. The company received an immediate order for 200 units before it had made a finalised system. This attempted theft was widely reported in the trade press and the company received 59 separate enquiries for the product, both from hirers and from companies wanting to offer a fitting service. Like it or not, it had a product!

Beta test results

Results came back fairly quickly from the different vehicles. Problems generally were small but could prove troublesome to the car owner.

Remedial actions

Carburettor and diesel injectors use a single fuel pipe from fuel tank to engine. Cars using fuel injectors have two pipes – a flow and return. On one vehicle, the stop valve was fitted into the return pipe in error, which appeared to work, but which would not have made the vehicle absolutely secure. The installation guides were changed, and it was decided to enclose photographs and a simple tracing guide from fuel tank to engine, so that the fitter could clearly identify the feed and return pipes.

Five vehicles were broken into during the test. None was stolen. In one, an attempt in daylight was made to bypass the fuel valve which was secured by 'screw-type jubilee clip'. It failed. In order to make it impossible for the clips to be unscrewed, the jubilee type clips were replaced with a security clip which required to be cut off, as it could not be undone once it was fastened. Three of the keyfob buttons were lost during the test. Replacements were despatched by post and worked without problems.

Customers' feedback

A number of important customer-related points came out of the test:

1 Private car owners liked the system and did not find the Touch memory system intrusive
2 Company car owners would have preferred the medium-cost RF tag system, as they found the Touch memory system a bit difficult to get used to. Spouses were often mentioned, who had had problems
3 All agreed the system was 'much better' than mechanical immobilisers
4 Fleet car managers indicated that they would be able to get lower insurance premiums, which would pay for the system and its fitting in the first year
5 Commercial van drivers found the Touch memory irksome, as they had a continual stop/start routine. Owner/drivers regarded the system as being very good value. Owner/drivers were divided as to whether they would spend additional money on the medium-cost system, even if it was easy to use in a stop/start regime

6 Commercial van owners would pay for the system instantly as the insurance premiums would fall by twice the cost of the system and fitting

7 Most of the drivers who fitted their own system took just over one hour. When asked if they would do it again most agreed that they would. It was regarded as straightforward. Most said that if fitting to the same car again they could do it in about 30 minutes. Three asked if they could fit them commercially!

8 When asked if they would like 'high profile' security stickers, they were split 50:50. Some felt it was a deterrent, while others felt that it would act as a challenge to potential thieves.

Fleet car users, who did not have to pay for the product, were more disposed to the medium-cost system. Car owners, or van owner drivers who paid for their system were far more inclined to express satisfaction with the Touch memory system. This clearly, was dependent on who paid for the product. It was decided to offer 'high profile' stickers with all products, which could be installed at the drivers' discretion.

The product was seen to be simple to fit by DIY. Trade fitters would find it very easy and probably would be able to offer a reliable fitting service in about 30 minutes. There were no obvious problems apart from the quality of documentation. It was decided to draw up simple installation tables so that fuel-injected, petrol-engined vehicles could have an additional check as to which fuel pipe was flow and which was return. The documentation would be accompanied by flow charts and photographs.

Product derivatives

Four lengths of wiring loom would be offered – short, medium, long and generic (for lorries and boats). Offered for sale to the retail sectors, the packaging would indicate length of the loom inside. Each pack would have a list of the popular cars and vans which it would fit. For trade sale it was decided to pack the units in packs of six. This would mean that the valve/Touch memory system would be in one box. Wiring looms would be packed in separate packs of six. This would allow the trade to keep simple stocks and mix and match.

Initial orders

After evaluation Mary obtained initial orders for both DIY retail sale and trade fitting, which exceeded the first two months' production capacity.

The team decided to increase production to meet these orders, but not to expand the order base immediately, in order to double check that the initial production was robust. The ease with which orders had come about, and the volumes, caused a rapid rewrite of the business plan and a further submission was made to the board.

In the submission to Gate 4 the team had asked for the cash to build the beta test product. In fact they had sold the product at cost, so that the board were impressed with the ease of sale and the subsequent sales. They agreed the passage of the product to full production, on the basis of a limited build-up of sales.

Gate 5

The build-up to commercial launch was taking place.

Market familiarity

Marketing and now Sales were able to start talking a sales roll out. At this stage certain unfamiliar practices started to cause problems. The multiple vehicle accessory distributors and major retailers wanted their own boxes, and also this required the unique barcode which retail operations need and require for EPOS operations. This took time and money to implement, simply because it was a strange process to a company that had not done it before. Luckily the team decided to employ an outside consultant on packaging and he was able to use his industry contacts to accelerate the process.

The production department was able to implement the computer software which Gurjit had devised without any modification and was able to work the production line almost straight away. Since the wiring loom required a single-colour conductor as an anti-tamper measure, the risk of miswired looms was high. Production produced a loom tester which rapidly checked the loom before the rest of the system was tested. Rejects were low in number.

The warehousing department was in a learning curve as the range of products was limited, but the range of different packaging and therefore part numbers was quite high, and again subject to human error. Meetings with production resulted in packing being directly off the end of the production line rather than the more normal company procedure of production into skips and subsequent packing. As the production of the in house components was campaign based it was possible to pack directly into prepared packaging, which meant that the tested item was packed directly after testing, so reducing the chances of human error.

Up until now, the outline business plan was the driving force. However, as a complete business plan it was lacking in many of the components which would have made it robust. Jane, a new trainee work accountant was seconded onto the team, and within two weeks had produced a far more robust plan, which more or less integrated all elements of the process and allowed the sales forecast to relate directly to both variable and fixed costs. It was found that the anticipated break-even point was some seven months later than anticipated. However, modest growth in the product would push profits much higher than previously predicted, specially if during the second year the production was switched from discrete components to ASICs. However, a faster sales uptake would almost compensate for the later break-even point. This point was discussed with the board. The team felt that a slower and controlled roll out was preferable to a faster and more risky process. The board agreed, specially as the second medium-cost product needed the same treatment once handover to production had taken place. In addition, once a critical volume had been reached, the economies of the ASIC would come into play. By then, experience would be good enough to put the entire circuitry of the low-cost product onto a single chip.

Company roll out – immmobilisers

The agreed process was that the first product to go on sale was the low-cost system based on Touch memory. When this was under way the team would do a better and more detailed beta test on the medium-cost system, having done more detailed testing on the ignition coil, modified to their patents. Once the medium-cost product was successfully launched, the next product would be the low-cost product with ASIC in place of discrete circuitry. By then turnover would be about £1.35m.

Patents and trademarks

R&D reported that from their provisional patent application, a search had indicated no prior art or any grey area in their patent application and that they should seriously consider a specific trademark for the product. The decided on Digilock, which was submitted as a trademark. As it is selling in the EC, it made a European patent application to protect that market.

Margaret, a young graduate trainee, was recruited to the team, with responsibility for training outside organisations to fit the product in a retail environment. She proved to be so effective as a trainer that orders quickly arrived from retailers even though a launch date had yet to be decided.

Pre-launch activity

Close working with the insurance industry had generated a lot of enthusiasm for the products. Trade enquiries were received even at Gate 3 stage. There was a need for a trade fitting service and many local companies wanted to be able to buy product to expand their vehicle security portfolio.

Insurance approvals scheme

It was decided to offer the medium-cost system for full appraisal and approval by the BIA testing station at Thatcham in Berkshire. The costs and time involved were offset by being formally approved, which in the 'upmarket and hot hatch' marketplace, would result in substantially discounted insurance. In addition, a major retail network, its main lines being exhausts and tyres, was looking for a new range of products to be fitted on demand. It examined the beta test product, and on the results of their testing added the low-cost ranges to its product portfolio.

Mary managed to link together two discrete partners as a marriage of convenience to the benefit of all parties. A major insurance company, its business being car insurance, specifically by telephone, wanted a product which could reduce car theft. Clearly, it could only encourage its clients to fit the product against a discount for fitting. It did not have any means of checking that the product had been installed, and if it was, that it had been done properly. Mary was able to put the company in touch with the nationwide chain, which gave the following advantages:

1 Guaranteed and professional fitting
2 Draw through strategy – insurance company could publicise the product/service with its renewal notices
3 Customer got a more secure car and at a lower premium
4 Nationwide chain got increased referral business with very little extra cost of sales
5 Manufacturer sold product on the back of this marriage of convenience.

Sales was unable to directly identify a company that could offer a nationwide fitting service in the truck or plant hire business. It was able however to contact sales agents that sold into that market. These agents sold to the larger fleets and so were able to introduce the product to that market. This was also quite extensively written about in the trade press. It was also able to identify two insurance companies that specialised in policies for that market, and were able to arrange a simple mainsheet to the insured users, which again relied on a special reduction in premium against the fitting of the product. In the case of a JCB digger, it was in the order of £600 ... more than the cost of the product and fitting.

COMMENT

*The product meets **Right Product** as it fills a niche in the market between alarms and low-cost mechanical immobilisers.*

*It meets **Right Time** criteria, simply because car theft is at record levels and insurance companies are desperate to reduce claims by offering incentives.*

*It meets **Right Production** criteria by being phased into different channels as production and market experience builds.*

*It meets **Right Price** by showing a payback against the insurance discount in the first year.*

*It meets **Right Position** in being the only digital low-cost immobiliser, more effective than an alarm at less cost.*

13

TAILORING THE SCHEME TO YOUR COMPANY

Basics

No two companies, even in the same industry are the same. Different styles of management and workforces will give different means of achieving the same objectives.

First decision

The first decision must be taken by the senior management or directors. The decision is simple: 'The company must improve its performance in bringing new products to market'. The roads to improvement must include a quick analysis of what is currently in place. If the company has a good record on new product development, both in terms of success rate and speed to market, then it would be foolish to make any major changes. Fine-tuning may be needed. If, on the other hand, the development record is poor, patchy or commercially successful, but later to market, then obviously major improvement is needed.

Next decision

The next decision is simple. Continue using the system we have used with modifications – or start again. Only the senior management can decide what is best.

Starting again may allow putting in place the climate of innovation within the company and call into question some of the more traditional ways of doing things. The way forward is to convene a meeting of senior managers from all departments, and to cold-bloodedly analyse the past record. The game plan is to identify as much as possible on past performance. The following need to be identified:

1 What the company does well, and consistently
2 What the company does passably well, but with some problems
3 What the company does inconsistently
4 What the company does badly.

For example, a company may have a history of producing a product well, but then finding that its target market was wrong. It may have sold better, in a different and non-targeted market. This indicates a lack of good market research and incorrect β testing.

From the outcome above, the meeting will have to decide the company strengths and weaknesses in the development of new products. From this work, the company must decide to modify the existing set-up or to start again. In doing so, it is often helpful to do a quick post mortem on a couple of past products, one that failed and one that succeeded. The 'compare and contrast' approach should allow the setting up of the new guidelines, to ensure that both success and failure would have been measured by whatever scheme is being used. The important question is: 'If the company implemented the New Product Scheme, would it have highlighted both the success and failure factors in the products examined?'

SETTING UP A NEW PRODUCT SCHEME

Task force

A small task force needs to be set up. It needs to be interdepartmental and of middle-ranked employees, who tend to know more than many senior managers about the nuts and bolts of the daily activities. The task force needs to identify how to implement and modify the basic New Products Scheme. The decision output from the meetings should include:

1 How many gates or review stages are needed
2 How to agree 'funding' as personnel, time, physical money, or even 'plant time' for experimentation
3 How to score the potential product for features/benefits.
4 What standard type of business plan to follow
5 What spreadsheet to use
6 To an extent, what external help can be called in as part of the development process
7 How to handle
   (a) Failed gate reviews

    (b) Failed α tests

    (c) Failed β tests

8 How to form a 'contract' between the 'product team' and the company

9 What members of the core team will comprise (any discipline)

10 How the 'team' is allowed to form and manage itself. Ground rules if necessary

11 What decisions the team is empowered with, and what need to be referred

12 Who is empowered to sanction product number changes (badge engineered products, own labels etc.)

13 How to do product number changes

14 The composition of the New Products Committee (disciplines, experience, status – not actual personalities)

15 Allocation of members' time from their department managers

16 An ombudsman to sort out disputes been departments, managers, or teams

17 How to handle informal approaches from individuals or embryonic teams.

This is before any product has been seen or put through the Scheme. This sets up the ground rules, which in the light of the first few products may need to be modified. The task force should then present its ideas to the company board of directors. The output of that meeting should be regarded as the first blueprint. Essentially it is a 'charter'.

Setting up the Scheme

Once a number of primary review or gates has been agreed, the task force needs to produce a modified version of Chapter 4 or 5. This should provide a sort of outline blueprint for any individual who may want to ask the company for funding. There should be another set of rules of engagement which should encompass the company's decisions above. These again may be modified in light of experience.

Training

All personnel should ultimately get a brief presentation on the Scheme itself, along with an established means for any member of staff to be able to make sensible suggestions, about either the job, or an idea that could be related to the company's activities. Bear in mind that this can be an ideal time to encourage a more innovative approach to innovation, and to get the entire workforce behind the concept.

All managers, should be trained in a much deeper way to understand the entire Scheme as implemented by the company. In addition, the managers should be taught that they must encourage their staff to propose new ideas, and that any such suggestions will be faithfully ascribed to the member of staff, and not to the department or the managers themselves. This is key to the encouragement of ideas. Original ideas must be ascribed to the inventor.

Problems

In most companies there are bound to be problems with this concept, specially if the company structure is traditional. They can be summarised:

1 The original idea needed to be 'worked up' into a useful and usable form
2 The manager plagiarises the original idea
3 One department 'hijacks' an idea from another
4 A team is credited with an idea of which came from an individual.

The company needs to try to change its managers' perspectives on management. 'It is easier to lead than to drive.' The mentor approach to the staff has a lot to commend it. For example, Reginald Mitchell, the designer of the Spitfire, one of the most outstanding warplanes of World War 2, used Alex Smith the chief designer as his protégé, and his entire staff in the drawing office at Supermarine. Mitchell tragically died before his new product had barely flown. However Alex Smith and his team turned the original product into some 47 different product variants, and are credited as producing a aircraft which had the distinction of being the only allied aircraft in production for the whole six-year war. Mitchell undoubtedly did both his company and his country great service and, by adopting the mentor approach, passed to his staff many of his thought processes, that would otherwise have died with him.

If managers can be motivated to promote their staff's ideas, then the process will move ahead at a pace. There are other quite profound side-effects. Many ideas will have no direct relevance to future products, but they will have profound effects on existing products. The fact that there is a channel for suggestions and ideas will enhance productivity because problems will be uncovered and eliminated by mutual management.

Selection of 'team members'

When an idea is developed the originator(s) will be seen to be in the core team. The team needs to be a balanced entity and this will require a certain amount of horse trading behind the scenes. Added to the originators must be other members of the team to give it balance, experience and drive.

Human nature, being what it is, will ensure that managers will be unhappy to allocate a member of staff's time to a project which is indefinable in terms of workload, or timescales. This means that they will have to understand the concept that new ideas do not come from a single department, and that to be developed properly they require the services of a dedicated few. It needs to be stressed that this process is in the interests of the company and its employees, however painful.

There are undoubtedly growing pains with every new scheme. This is why there needs to be a written 'charter' agreed by the board of directors. Over time these growing pains will go away, specially once the first successful product is launched. Most traditional managers will, in retrospect, admit both reservations in the process and selfishness on their part in their staff's time.

Encouragement

There can be little doubt that Japanese working practices are highly effective. One feature of their management style is the ability of the company workers to meet in an interdepartmental way, and to receive information from both within and external to the company. These briefing sessions act as a trigger to innovation. The more brains considering an idea, the greater the chance of a good idea coming forward and making a good product. For example, much is made of the Japanese 'consensus approach to decision taking'. This is no more than a group of diverse individuals, given the same problem, formulating within each of them, more or less the same solution.

If regular meetings on an informal basis can be set up, the better the flow of information between departments hence improved understanding of how the departments works and the problems they face. Such ideas are 'coffee and buns' at a given time each week and allow an informal meeting where there are no ground rules. Any topic related to the company can be discussed and in the early stages of such meetings it helps if there is a chairperson just to start off the proceedings. As time goes on, such a catalyst is not needed. Unlikely collaboration results, which indicates that the process is working.

Approach

An individual or group should be allowed to approach the company with an idea. Such a process must not be intimidatory but should be friendly and informal. The company may need to appoint one person as the 'administrator of ideas' so that the sanity check stage can take place informally. If the individual has not got the necessary partners to form an embryonic team he needs help to get the right co-partners to advance the idea, even to the sanity check stage. In such instances, it may be that the team needs only one other individual who can provide experience or skills that the proposer lacks. This is clearly different with each case. The important points are that the company should regard the ideas flow as being the start to new products, or the building of better existing ones. The process should not become inflexible, nor should it be time-consuming.

For example, the system needs to understand how a sanity check will be informally processed before a Gate 1 review. Normally a member of the New Products Committee would act as mentor, to screen the process and help the embryonic team in a situation that may be totally unfamiliar. The system needs to be thorough and it needs to consume as little time as possible, as there should be a number of different sanity checks that need screening. It would be quite wrong that the time of the whole New Products Committee was spent on each sanity check. A nominated member should be quite enough. In the sanity checking stage, the NPC member, should allow the free flow of ideas to other departments, so that a better and more rounded potential product is achieved.

Experience

Each company is a live entity. Each company is different. As time goes on, once the process has started it will become more natural and less forced. Experience will allow better and faster decisions and managers will be able to make better informed decisions based on previous experience of the Scheme. The end result of the Scheme should be better, more successful products. This means the continued prosperity of the company and its employees.

APPENDIX:
Answers to Worked Examples

Note: The answers given here are not exhaustive. There is do doubt that many other issues can be teased out. However, the issues below should allow the product plan, market research plan, and R&D plan to be formulated and for a decision to be reached.

Chapter 3

Situation 1 – Goldwell Chemical Co. Ltd

Question 1

1 For how long does it work before the efficiency reduces?
2 Are the costs really that good?
3 What combinations of metals have been tried?
4 What are the potential licence fees?
5 Any idea of manufacturing costs?
6 Any idea of economic volumes initially?
7 Can silicon makers come down in price if needs be? If so how far?
8 If the product reduces electricity costs what new markets will develop and on what timescales?
9 2 methyl ferrichrome is a new compound. Any health issues? Ames test results?

Question 2

With a market worth £100m to £2bn, anybody stopping the project at this stage needs to be shot!

Situation 2 – Foster & Small

1 Estimated market size worldwide and estimated size it may be able to service
2 Any patents problems – is the alloy patentable/trademark protectable?
3 What effect on the cost of the lock (would manufacturers accept the extra costs?)

4 Can the new alloy be cast in the same way as the old?
5 Is the proposed alloy as strong as is claimed? (Very good lead into the funding that is needed)
6 Will this increase Foster & Small's market share? If so by how much?
7 What are the production implications – will new plant be needed?
8 As well as fitting to new cars, could the lock be retrofitted to older cars?
   – what is the market size?

Chapter 6

Situation 1 – Parry & Brown Ltd

1 **Test the waters** Paul needs to establish whether the P & B clientele actually *likes* the product. He should either buy a unit from Holland, or make one in PVC; also build a similar product in wood and put them on display at a few shows to gauge customer reaction and comment. The output from this simple consumer test will indicate a preference for either one or the other, or neither!

2 **Outline business plan** After customer comments he should look at the costs, margins and proposed sales prices of his various options. He should then write a very simple business plan so that senior management can look at the reward versus risk factor with a view to allocating time and money. He should produce a simple sales forecast and roughly cost out the options, with regard to volume manufacture, buy price and sell price. Luckily he has the Dutch product which gives him a rough idea of what the market will tolerate.

   As he is using a new material, he should draw up a clear list of advantages and disadvantages, so that he can sell the product to his senior management. The advantages/disadvantages analysis should include both the customer benefits and the P & B perspective in terms of buying, machining, and selling the new material.

3 **Further research** He should talk to a supplier of polyurethane foam with a view to visiting a mast maker, in order to find out how to inject the foam and what sort of difference it will make. He will need to put in place a simple mechanical testing regime so that he can then decide what is acceptable and what is not.

4 **Design** He may wish to consider a different design which may 'cantilever' the upright beams to reduce the bending moments.

5 **Actions** In any event Paul needs his team to do a number of things:
   (a) What effect will the new pergola have on traditional sales?
   (b) Can it be sold in the same way?
   (c) Can it be sold in a different way as well – by mail order for situation?
   (d) How will it compare to wood in terms of longevity?
   (e) Materials costings with the different supply options
   (f) Working/production costs
   (g) What sort of profit margin can the market bear?
   (h) Consideration of design or trademark protection?
   (j) Will the product be supplied and fitted like the wooden ones, or could it be DIY?
   (k) If the latter, does this open up new sales channels? If so, what are the margins.
   (l) Should several samples be made and field tested with real customers?
   (m) If plastics are viable what tools/equipments will he need? At what cost? Timescales?
   (n) Does the plastics version open a different market from the traditional wood, and does this mean different customers, sales channels and sales methods. Can other products be sold similarly?

Situation 2 – Anders and Weightell Ltd

Question 1

1 What is the predicted growth in the cap business in the UK. Any export?
2 How does A & W expect to position itself?
3 What is the future for metal caps? Is the market shrinking? If so, how much?
4 Is there an outline business plan with differing growth rates?
5 Any chance of metal caps being outlawed by supermarkets?
6 What are the competitors doing?
7 Are there any industries which require metal caps and exclude plastics, for safety etc.?

Question 2

1 Continue with metal caps exclusively
2 Operate a joint metal and plastics enclosure policy
3 Wind down metals and move to plastics

4 What are the niche markets which the above policies may exclude? Net worth?

5 Can A & W learn plastics processing? What timescale? What entry cost?

6 Can A & W enlist an external co-partner in plastics, but not in the packaging business?

7 What effect would a co-partner have on profits?

8 Could A & W purchase a plastic processing business complete? If so, how much?

Question 3

1 Write outline business plan with options and 'what if' scenarios

2 Identify plastics companies that could be co-partners – sound them out

3 Identify small plastics companies with view to purchase. How much?

4 Initiate market research interviews with industry consultants with regard to the future of metal and plastic caps. Also get sales to identify any niche markets which may not be able to use plastic caps. Talk to customers in these markets to understand their problems. Speak to editors of trade magazines for their views. Any conservation issues?

5 Obtain capital costs for purchase of relevant injection moulding machines.

6 Costs of hiring both plastics consultant and senior experienced plastics processing manager

7 Costs of the R&D required to make plastics enclosures. Costs of loss of market if company do not embrace plastics (e.g. lost sales, lost market share in longer term)

8 Outline action plan, who is involved, what timescales and working hours. Costs of salaries and expenses

9 Indication of how long the learning curve would take and how soon revenue could be expected from plastics if this route is adopted

10 Revisit the relative net profit margins of both metal and plastics.

Situation 3 – Capital and Municipal Assurance Co.

Question 1

1 Large potential market for finance products

2 'One stop shop' for house, mortgage, life assurance, buildings and contents insurance

3 Large database of property-owning, responsible citizens to sell other products to – car and pensions etc.
4 Economies of scale – lower costs and better customer service
5 Self-financing – profits from estate agencies would fund the merger into a corporate whole
6 Nationwide chain to help with company moves from anywhere in the country
7 Tied-in legal service and conveyancing
8 Large capital base which is likely to appreciate over time – property prices usually go up.

Question 2

1 Strengths that:
   (a) Economies of scale
   (b) One stop shop
   (c) Large chain with 'blue chip' name, easily identifiable
   (d) Captive customer base.

2 Weaknesses:
   (a) Property market prone to changes in economy
   (b) Whole strategy based on house sales – if they stop, so does the revenue stream
   (c) Financial regulations in the future may require consumer choice
   (d) Merging estate agency and insurance company culture may be hard
   (e) Capital values of property owned/leased by chain may go down if there is a recession
   (f) Consumers may actually like the freedom of choice.

Question 3

1 Continue with present strategy
2 Create a stronger tie with independent estate agents
3 Consider a 'test market' of a comprehensive package to the independents with sales incentives
4 Purchase lists of householders and do direct marketing of the proposed products by mail
5 Consider a telephone direct line business and tie it in with the above mailshots
6 Establish an outline business plan and cost it for the establishment of a nationwide chain and costs/profits. Then work through same plan using

existing sales channels and add proposed new alternatives and costs/profits

7 Approach other property-based companies such as banks and mortgage lenders, which are not identified as being a competitor and establish if it is possible to market an innovative product range via themselves.

Situation 3 – Polders & Sons

Question 1

1 The existing sales provide a clue as to the demand
2 That demand should assume stocking 365 days/year
3 That some sort of promotion should take place. What effect will that have?
4 If a licensing agreement could be agreed, what European demand could be added?

Question 2

1 The company will have to 'take a view' as to the ingredients needed and cost
2 Can existing plant be used or will new be required?
3 Can their present packaging system handle the product? If not what is needed/how much?
4 What could be the payback time for new equipment if it is needed?
5 What volume changes could the production department tolerate if the product succeeds?

Question 3

1 This is a classic situation where only experience will tell
2 Are there any previous products that have been promoted? What was the increase in sales?
3 Is the product an impulse buy? Seasonal (Christmas)? Would branding make an important difference?

Question 4

This should be answered by the sales and marketing department, which should know if there is a competitor, and if unsure, know whom to talk to in order to obtain the information.

Question 5

1 The marketing department must clearly know the buy-in prices and the mark-ups

2 Production must be able to fairly accurately cost the raw materials and overheads

3 The only variable here will be the volumes, and the effect that larger volumes might have on the overall costs

4 The other questions that needs to be answered are, whether the UK-made product can be sold at a price differential; whether higher labour costs are offset by no shipping costs; what effect the proposed advertising budget will have. In other words, what will the market bear?

Chapter 7

Situation 1

Question 1

In this instance the decision is probably one of 'hold' on the shelving project and 'go' on the fence spike. The reasons are as follows:

1 The moderate requirements of the spike product mean short-term revenue

2 No new capital injections or learning curves are needed

3 The sales are assured for the spike – not so for the plastic shelving

4 The shelving project has not really quantified the opportunity in terms of profit

5 Nothing in the shelving project suggests that a move from steel to plastic is urgent or that existing business will suffer in the short term

6 The company would be better served by putting its limited resources into the spike project as it will produce near immediate benefits. The shelving can wait until the spike project has been passed to production.

Situation 2

Question 1

1 You need to assume at this stage that your proposed upmarket store will move considerably more videos and provide a second revenue stream from CD ROMS and computer software

2 You should conduct some sort of basic survey of high street retailers to

establish that there are no competitors

3 You should research the other sales channels accordingly indicating margins and direct and indirect costs

4 You should have contacted a number of estate agents in commercial property and obtained facts and figures from them

5 You should talk to potential software distributors under a secrecy agreement, bearing in mind that the immature state of the CD ROM market means that different distributors are involved as compared with conventional software

6 You should initiate some serious consumer research into the habits of the video hiring population. This could be by high street interviews and separate focus groups. You need to establish that they will value your more extensive video-hiring selection and also that they would be interested in CD ROMS and computer software. It is quite possible that the groups who go looking to buy CD ROMS may be different to those who hire videos. It may also be important to understand the video-hiring mentality, so that you may be able to establish whether a more expensive hire cost might be offset against a wider selection. You may also like to find out whether the potential clients would prefer their store to be in a secondary location, rather than in direct high street locations. Clearly the site location is key. Parking may be a major issue. From these interviews you should be able to establish a customer profile

7 You should consider doing some market research in the US. You may be able to find some published work and you may also be able to interview the US chains whose idea you are plagiarising. You may also be able to suggest some idea of a joint venture or franchise operation. You might also consider conducting similar US consumer interviews to those in the UK. These should output a US customer profile. You would therefore be able to compare and contrast the attitudes of both US and UK consumers. You should try to obtain figures for turnover/sq. metre in $ for straight video rental stores, and for combined. This would again give you some idea of what you should be aiming for

8 You should then write a sample business plan based on the information you have. This should allow you to 'model' a single store, work out the volumes necessary for profitable operation and the payback period for fitting out costs etc. Your model should include pricing changes and 'special offers' to entice people to your store

9 Based upon your work, you should try to get the company to agree to a simple one-site trial and to sanction the costs involved. This test must

be equated to the α test. There will be an interesting learning curve here and once the viability of the first store is established it will be possible to fairly quickly duplicate the model in different locations.

Chapter 8

Situation – Goldwell Chemical Co.

Question 1

1 What comparison tests have been carried out with competitor cells? Results
2 How do costs sq. metre/watt compare with competition?
3 Can product be improved further? What timescales? Is outside help needed? If so, what?
4 Has accelerated ageing been done? How does it compare with competition?

Question 2

1 What external tests have been conducted by interested parties? Results?
2 Identify at least five 'typical customers'
3 What would be their likely purchase rate?
4 How would they use the product differently to the silicon cell?
5 With lowered cost where would they find new markets? How large?
6 Are there any 'sunrise' technologies which would use the device? Any technological interaction?
7 What are the strengths and weaknesses of the cells compared with competition?
8 What are the predicted costs of the development programme? What timescales?
9 What are the updated revenue forecasts? How does production view the possibilities?
10 Would production be in house or by a third party? How long the learning curve?
11 Some heavy metals are highly toxic. What health, safety, transport and consumer rules apply? Any EC, customs or other rules which may be applied? What tests need to be conducted? Is an expert consultant needed?

Question 3

1 Gaunt should present alternative scenarios with regard to establishing licensees and:
   - Likely licensing fees per annum
   - Likely guesstimated sales of chemical ingredients
   - Likely number of licensees
   - Strategy policy with regard to numbers and geography of licensees
   - Costs of this approach in terms of setting-up costs, and loss of end user profits
   - Time to market.

2 Likely costs of establishing production and going it alone:
   - Cost of plant
   - Cost of labour
   - Cost of learning how to make, test and ship the product
   - Cost of sales in an alien market
   - Possible co-partners
   - Estimated uptake rates – low, medium and high
   - Time to market.

3 The above should be put into a simple business plan, and should be extrapolated over 2, 5, 10 and 20 years to see the payback potential for both alternatives.

Question 4

1 **Marketing**
   - Establish potential co-partners for sales
   - Identify any 'sunrise' technologies
   - Establish outline pricing and apply to business plan
   - Identify real customers. Arrange confidentiality agreement with view to testing α samples
   - Identify competitor technologies – existing and potential new applications. Estimate volumes
   - Research potential licensee partners with geography (if needed)
   - Co-operate to write outline business plan.

2 **R&D**
   - Initiate health and safety audit. Research major world markets for legislation affecting transport and use of materials. Find out what

clearance testing is needed. Check major customs legislation world-wide. Use trade/DTI sources. Identify consultant if needed
- Write out safety test plan with timings and personnel
- Arrange further ageing tests as needed
- Co-operate to write outline business plan.

3 Production
- Indicate likely suppliers of bought-in components
- Indicate likely plant/equipment for assembly of cells. Order lead times. Costs
- Indicate likely personnel needs with timings, cost and training
- Indicate likely safety needs. Write statement
- Indicate likely 'learning curve' to full quality and robust production
- Write proposed quality testing procedures and establish techniques if needed
- Co-operate to write outline business plan.

4 Finance
- Work with all departments to produce outline business plan
- Produce simple computer model assuming varying growth rates. Indicate payback terms based on varying timescales
- Compare cost/reward factors to a licensing regime as compared with 'go it alone'
- Establish risk/reward factors for both treatments
- Use best estimates of growth rates in new and existing markets.

Question 5

The business plan should be able to run a series of 'what if' scenarios to tease out of the system the critical factors involved. It should clearly be able to quantify the risk/reward factors, the likely development costs, the options of licensing versus 'go it alone' and the various cash flow problems which would naturally result.

As this is a new product in a new market, there should be as many best guesses as possible. However, some means of forecasting may be needed, so that a number of different growth rates and market share options should be included. A competitor technology may emerge which may radically alter the projected market share. Very conservative estimates should be used, and the production issues should allow for very much slower, or faster, uptake and how the system would respond.

Chapter 9

Situation 1 – Andrews & Porlock Ltd

Question 1

1 The temptation is always to pursue the new avenue regardless. A & P should stick with the existing market that they know. The new market is likely to be a small niche inside a larger market overall. It may be very profitable, but only if the production of the product exists and the development costs are spread over a large number of units
2 The team should invest time in quantifying the new potential market
3 The team should consider producing a 'product variant' aimed at that market with name change, higher margins and differing sales channel.

Question 2

There is no reason to make any changes. A member of sales or marketing and a member from the technical team should spend some time in the field discussing their new innovation with potential customers. From that they should draw up a module to the business plan, giving scope to this niche market. They should attempt to sell the existing proposed product with as little change as possible, with correct functionality in the new niche market. They should quantify potential sales numbers, margins, sales channels and user benefits. The new module should be added to the business plan.

Question 3

The only additional actions are to quantify the new business opportunity. The old opportunity is unchanged. Continue to work on the agreed course. The new opportunity will only add cream on the top of the cake!

Chapter 10

Question 2

1 The product should be put into limited commercial manufacture
2 The product should be given to mixed ability groups in competitive shooting conditions and scored against competitors, in such a way that all groups use all weapons, in the same conditions
3 The product should be given to field units and tested in a complex variety of climatic and water-based conditions. Records should be kept

of field conditions and failures, both of the new product and the product it is to replace

4 Armourers would be expected to make comments on any failures of either weapon

5 Statistical sampling should be used and the results should indicate that the product is better than the rifle it replaces, in at least five features/benefits

6 There should be random sample interviews with users of the production model and comparisons with other weapons they have used. These should be conducted without fear or favour.

Question 3

It is expected to be the main rifle of the UK forces into the next century, therefore it should be able to perform better than the AK47, which is showing its age. If it is not acceptable, the product must be recycled, and put back to Gate 3 for redesign. If this is not possible the product should be cancelled.

Chapter 11

Situation – Dither & Scrattchet's mistake

This is every director's worst nightmare! The company has done everything right and now at the launchpad, the whole product is put on hold. Your options are:

1 Go ahead – launch product and risk being sued for patent infringement
2 Stop the launch – redesign the entire system to remove the infringement
3 Stop the project completely
4 Come to some arrangement with the patent holder.

In order to help the decision-making process the product team should be looking at:

1 Redesigning the product – costs – timescales, cost of lost market share, cost of production tooling etc.
2 Cost of stopping the project completely – lost market, lost sales, lost development costs
3 Cost of licensing the patent – if the patent holder will do so
4 Potential costs of patent infringement and subsequent 'desist' order.

From the work done it should be possible to get a scale of costs, time-scales and lost business; from that a critical path. Obviously the easiest path is the licensing of the patent from the other holder if he will grant it. Such costs could be put down to the patent agents' indemnity insurance! This would only delay the launch by a few weeks, but clearly is dependent on the goodwill and understanding of the patent holder.

Sanity check

1 **Idea**   Can it be ... ?
   - Patented
   - Copyrighted
   - Trademarked
   - Incorporated into existing products
   - New product
   - Licensed.

1 **Markets**   Existing ... new ... both?
   - Approximate size
   - Expanding or contracting?
   - Competition
   - Comparative costs of competition
   - If new route to market, any joint venture, alliance?

3 **Utility**   Why will customers buy?
   - List features and benefits
   - Crude idea of make cost
   - Can it be made using existing resources? If not what is needed?
   - What will influence the product?
     - Market drivers   - 'Fashion'
     - Regulations   - Efficiency
     - New technologies   - Cost
     - Competitors   - Performance

4 **Other**   What effect on existing range?
   - Enhance
   - Compete
   - New markets?

BIBLIOGRAPHY

Allen, David *Developing Successful New Products*, Pitman Publishing, 1994

Birn, Robin *The Effective Use of Market Research*, Kogan Page

Birn, Robin *Using Marketing Research to Grow Your Business*, Pitman Publishing, 1994

Blackwell, Edward *How to Prepare a Business Plan*, Kogan Page, 1993

Cooper, Robert G. *Winning at New Products*, Kogan Page, 1988

Holt, *Product Innovation Management*, 1988

Housden, Mathew *Successful Market Research in a Week*, Hodder & Stoughton, 1992

Kraushar, Peter M. *Practical Business Development*, Holt, Rinehart & Winston, 1985

Thomas, Michael (ed.) *Marketing Handbook*, Gower, 1988

INDEX